How to Survive  Divorce

Splendid

PUBLICATIONS

Anthea Turner

For all my friends
and family who've
picked me up,
dusted me down
and put me back on
my feet again.

How To Survive Divorce
By Anthea Turner

Splendid Publications Ltd
Unit 7
Twin Bridges Business Park
South Croydon
Surrey CR2 6PL

www.splendidpublications.co.uk

British Library Cataloguing in Publication Data is available from The British Library

ISBN: 9781909109735

Designed by Chris Fulcher at Swerve Creative Design & Marketing Ltd.
www.swerve-creative.co.uk

Printed and bound by CPI Group (UK) Ltd., Croydon, CR0 4YY

Commissioned by Shoba Vazirani

Every effort has been made to fulfil requirements with regard to reproducing
copyright material. The author and publisher will be glad to rectify any omissions
at the earliest opportunity.

Rear jacket image: Alison Webster

Contents

How to Survive Divorce

Blissfully happy on my wedding day... who knew what lay ahead.

Introduction

July 17th 2013 is a beautiful day. The sun is shining, the sky is cloudless and it's pleasantly warm. I've left the heat, noise, and artificial light of the London Underground at Chancery Lane and am now soaking in the afternoon sunlight as I slowly make my way through the City streets.

I stare at buildings as I walk. It's a passion of mine imagining what went on behind these huge oak doors when they were first hung in the eighteen hundreds. But really I'm not concentrating; my mind is all over the place, pictures of my life are flicking through my head and I'm clutching too tightly to a large file that contains details of what I know of my finances.

The street I've now reached is Bedford Row, the encampment of Britain's brightest legal brains. The picture which is sticking in my head more than the others is one taken on my wedding day almost thirteen years ago. There I am, sitting on a horse on a carousel with the man who has swept me off my feet, promised me the earth and made me feel like the luckiest woman in the world. If only I could speak to that blissfully happy woman and tell her what was going to happen...But there would be no point, she wouldn't believe me, she's lost in the moment.

I turn and walk up a set of steps and ring the buzzer. There are tears dripping from my eyes onto the York Stone below; I'm a mess. I'm fifty-three and today instead of working out what's for tea I'm filing for divorce from Grant Bovey. I'm here to speak to my lawyer about ending my life as I know it; to legally disassociate myself from the man I have loved for nearly fifteen years and believed with all my heart I would grow old with.

Nearly four years on from that sad day I'm in a healthier, more optimistic frame of mind but it's taken every hour of every one of those years and a serious amount of hard work to rediscover my independence, confidence, and inner strength. Only now do I feel I've returned to the person I am and somewhat shocked when I recollect a woman I don't recognise, whose normality slowly became a co-dependent, people-pleasing wreck, sacrificing her own independent mind through fear of loneliness and of losing everything she'd invested her love in. This woman was so intent on keeping the family unit together to the point of forgiving her husband his infidelity that she totally forgot herself.

In writing and researching this book, I have spoken to many experts in their fields who have kindly agreed to contribute where necessary, offering their wisdom. They have been incredibly generous with their time and any errors are definitely mine, not theirs.

I have also spoken to many amazing women who've been through divorce and come out the other side, a little battered and bruised perhaps but definitely stronger for the experience. They've also been kind enough to share their stories. Where requested, their names have been changed to protect their privacy.

I make no apologies when I say this book is aimed at women, particularly women of a 'certain age'. When I was looking for comfort in the pages of endless self-help books, I couldn't find exactly what I was hoping for; that book hadn't been written. Hopefully this will go some way towards helping other women who find themselves in the same position I did.

My dreams of 'happily ever after' shattered.

Chapter One
The Olympic Split

Between the opening and closing of the London 2012 Olympics, my marriage was in tatters after I discovered Grant was having an affair, then restored to what I believed was honeymoon happiness. Watching the Rio Olympics on TV in 2016, I found it difficult to believe it had been four years since that tumultuous time.

Of course as is well-documented, my relationship with Grant was founded on adultery on both sides, a fact that I never allowed myself to forget. When we got together, he was already married to Della and parents to three lovely girls: Lily, Amelia and Claudia. I was married to former DJ and businessman Peter Powell. We didn't end our marriages lightly; ours was never simply a casual affair. But inevitably, breaking up two homes had painful consequences. What it taught me was that so many mistakes were made and people were hurt, something I've apologised for time and time again. I knew, without any shadow of a doubt, I would walk over broken glass to avoid it happening ever again.

When Grant once attempted to justify himself and silence my pain by saying he'd done it before, I was the 'other woman' and hadn't cared about his ex-wife Della's feelings, I was livid. It's such an easy justification but so wrong. I know I made mistakes — I freely and with all my heart apologise for them — but to move through life with intelligence you have to learn from them.

"Your last mistake is your best teacher."
– Ralph Nader

A red mist descended upon me as I realised what he'd done.

❤❤❤

Before I learned for sure Grant had been unfaithful, I felt something was amiss. I knew this man so well and sensed a change in him. His pattern of behaviour altered and he began staying away from our home in Surrey, preferring to overnight in London more and more. I didn't want to believe anything was wrong of course but I couldn't shake the feeling he was hiding something from me. I would question him and receive implausible explanations which I simply didn't buy, yet he made me feel I was in the wrong, being unnecessarily suspicious. This was my best friend, my partner, lover and confidant acting oddly, yet telling me I was imagining it. It's a horrible, horrible feeling when that happens and you can slowly feel your confidence eroding away. It destroys you from the inside out. Every time I asked him if there was anything the matter or why he was doing something I thought was a bit unusual, he'd give me an exasperated look and deny there was a problem until I started to change into a person I didn't want to be, giving him even more ammunition to behave like a man I didn't really know any more. I was left feeling vulnerable and exposed, totally different from the confident, happy woman he'd first met and fallen in love with.

Now, call me naïve but despite my sixth sense telling me my husband was acting out of character, I imagined all sorts of scenarios to explain his behaviour but infidelity was the last possibility on my long list. Common sense told me that it would be absolutely ridiculous for either of us to go down that path again. How wrong was I? The opening ceremony of the Olympics was knocked off the front page of the *Daily Mail* by sordid revelations of my husband's affair.

They often say that the 'wife is always the last to know,' but fortunately in my case, I wasn't quite last. Small comfort. The husband of one of my best friends, the former GMTV weather presenter Sally Meen, knew what was going on and Sally, a woman you truly want on your side, managed to pin him down and confess every detail to her. I needed to know the truth, however painful. At least I was semi-prepared before it all broke in the media, not that it lessened the pain...

The other woman

Everything came to a head in 2012 but unbeknown to me, the cracks in our marriage began to appear as far back as 2010 when things were not working out for Grant business-wise. I've always worked, it wasn't new to me but after taking more of a backseat to nurture our family, I had to step up to the plate once more as it looked as though Grant was facing bankruptcy. So when I got asked to screen

My beautiful dog Buddie during one of our many moves. He packed his bed and his brother.

Me in Canada sitting on our mobile dressing room and office.

test for a programme in Canada called *Dinner Party Wars*, I couldn't refuse. I flew out to Toronto where the show was filmed, for the shoot and later learned I had the job which couldn't have come at a better time for us financially. I'd already done bits and pieces such as panto to help pay the bills and we'd moved from our lovely family home, the sort dreams are made of, where I once filmed *Perfect Housewife*, into a smaller house in Hascombe, Surrey, to help reduce our outgoings.

I filmed the pilot of *Dinner Party Wars* and went on to make three series of the show. It wasn't too bad a journey and while I was over there, they looked after me beautifully.

I enjoyed the experience and it meant I was adding to the coffers while Grant was dealing with his problems. Life was chaotic and pressurised during this time but I did what I had to do. I'm a girl from the Midlands and when the going gets tough you roll your sleeves up and get on with it.

But while I was away from home, Grant by his own admission has since said to me 'I made a few bad judgements' and ones that were difficult to rectify once made. He had met a young girl who would go on to invade our lives and I knew nothing about it. I was thousands of miles away in Canada, oblivious that my husband was leading a double life. We spoke every day without fail and I was none the wiser. He was saying lovely things to me to keep me sweet. By nature I'm not a nosey parker, I'd never looked at another person's computer or 'phone or checked their bank statements. I'm trusting as a rule and while I did notice changes in Grant, it was all put down to the stresses of his bankruptcy. That explanation went on for two years! I felt sorry for what he was going through but I trusted him implicitly so I didn't suspect it was anything else causing the change in him.

Whenever I flew home from Toronto, everything was normal apart from the stress you'd expect from your partner's business collapsing. This was my best friend, my life partner, my husband and I was only ever supportive to him during this time. We went through so much to be together, it would never, ever, ever have occurred to me that he would be unfaithful, for practical reasons, never mind emotional reasons. We were so closely linked together; it would be the most ridiculous thing ever to start pulling it apart.

Because of our financial problems, we moved yet again, this time to a much smaller property in nearby Esher.

We kept moving home to reduce our living and running costs. We got rid of lots of overheads, which allowed us to live a simpler life. We managed to work it so that moving fell between filming series two and three of *Dinner Party Wars*. (At one point during this period we even looked at a house abroad and we seriously considering relocating. I'd measured up, done the floor plan, researched shipping and even worked out how to get my horse Caramelo freighted over.) Yet all the while, Grant was having an affair and I was totally blind to it, working, worrying and supporting my husband whose property business had come crashing down around his ears.

Of course there were already rumours circulating. Grant had apparently been spotted out with this woman – someone thought she was his daughter. On another occasion, they bumped into someone who knew me while they were out together and he introduced her as his niece! I was miles from home thinking I was helping while all the while, this woman had been in three of my homes, played with my dogs, cats, stared at pictures of the girls on the walls...She stepped into my nest, slept in my beds. I understand hotel rooms and cars but not another woman's nest; you've got to be brazen to do that. Literally as my car left for the airport, she arrived. I learned this from my gardener who admitted he hadn't had the heart to tell me at the time.

When Sally broke the news of Grant's affair to me, I couldn't move at first, I was in such shock. Physically, emotionally and mentally stunned. For twenty-four hours I did nothing. Grant went to a hotel while I sat at home in a catatonic state. The only person I spoke to was a friend of Grant's called Madoc Bellamy. I don't know what I'd have done without him at the end of the 'phone. My mind was on the chess board of life thinking of all the moves and all the people this was going to affect. I was frightened by what lay ahead: the train was on the wrong track and heading into carnage and I was powerless to sort this one out. It went dark but I didn't put the lights on. I got in the car and drove to my horse a mile away and sat still in the dark covered in shavings, glad of his warm body and his soothing noise as the sinking-in process took place. I couldn't face seeing anyone, I didn't trust anyone and my faithful horse who never let me down, gave me much-need solace. I don't remember being angry at this point, I was just numb. This happens to people all the time but I kept thinking not us and not this way after everything we've been through. But Grant had done the unimaginable and I was left to deal with the fall-out of his actions: the effect on our family, friends, finances and the hungry media.

We'd been together nearly fifteen years at this point,

Dancing to Puppy Love
on Dancing on Ice.

married for almost twelve, which is a long time. I thought we were solid and I was shattered to discover he clearly hadn't felt the same way. Yes Grant and I previously behaved badly too. For three months I lied to Peter. I hated myself for it as he's one of the dearest people I know but there were problems in our marriage and by then, we were just friends. I'm not justifying anything, I deceived and lied to him for three terrible months before coming clean. My affair with Grant was the catalyst to the end of our marriage which would have ended regardless. It was such an awful, painful time that I would never, ever do it again to anyone. I'm so damaged by it that if I feel a friend is turning onto that

Mauritius - still not been on a proper holiday since. Must sort.

hazardous road to hell, I attack their plan with everything I've got, convincing them it's the wrong and cowardly way to finish a marriage. But the hard fact is Grant lied to me for three years and now looking back I think that's the hardest thing I've found to get over. I often find myself quoting Gloria Hunniford who said to me, 'It's not the act it's the deceit.' So true.

Lawyers will tell you how difficult divorce is when there's someone else involved. Why would you want to do it? We had all worked so hard to build this family which began from infidelity, why would you want to do it again? As the girls articulated, 'You did it to Mum and now you've done it to Anthea. Why?'

When someone is doing something wrong and they know it, they need to justify their actions so they look for fault in the obstacle between them and their goal. 'Sorry' had become my most used word; anything and everything I did was wrong. I am - in therapy speak - a facilitator for bad behaviour because I will always try and sort, smooth and be the first to say 'Sorry, what have I done wrong?'

So before he was rumbled, I had apparently committed a string of misdemeanours from the time I would spend making Sunday lunch, my hatred for loud music in the house (I have ears like a bat), the way I put suntan lotion on (I burn big time) to the fact I apparently didn't party hard enough...the list was endless but instead of telling him to sod off, I lost my confidence and turned into a person I no longer knew. I was confused, bit my tongue and tried to do better, tried to make him happy. I just couldn't work out why this fifty-two year-old man was behaving so badly and saying such bizarre things. He even bought a sports car and wanted to go to Ibiza! When I eventually learned that the 'other woman' was just twenty-four – not much older than Grant's eldest daughter – it all made perfect sense. It wasn't me at all, it was him and I was stuck between incredulity and the hilarity of the text-book situation I found myself in.

I've already stated I'm a path smoother, always looking for the simple way through a problem, I'm a doer, a fixer, it's been my method of survival. I wouldn't blame anyone in the same position to just throw in the towel but I deeply valued the life we'd built together. The girls were as much a part of my life as they were their Dad's and they depended on us for so much, I couldn't let their lives be ripped apart without a fight so somehow we carried on communicating.

Grant quickly began to realise the consequences of his actions. The girls were in angry tears of frustration and disbelief. Mutual friends whom he respected and members of his family kept asking him what he was playing at. He became scared at the havoc he'd wreaked and it dawned on him how much he'd hurt me and his daughters. It took actually leaving me to make him wake up to what he stood to lose.

He wrote me letters and did everything he could to convince me he was truly sorry and that I was the love of his life and couldn't live without me. I of course still loved him and desperately wanted to believe him. So I did.

By the time the Olympics were over, so was Grant's affair and we were a couple again. I'd had to work incredibly hard on myself to forgive him but bearing in mind how much we both had to lose and how remorseful he appeared to be, I felt our marriage was worth saving and took him back. Our twelfth wedding anniversary that August could not have been more romantic. Around that time I was invited to take part in ITV1's *Dancing on Ice* and Grant persuaded me it was a great idea and a chance for me to do something for myself. Training for the show began in October and he was there for me every step of the way, tweeting me encouraging messages of support, telling everyone who would listen how well I was doing. He would bring the girls along to the rink to watch me practice and spur me on, sending flowers and making me feel so special and loved throughout the whole experience. I honestly felt our marriage was stronger than it ever had been.

That December we had a magical early Christmas with the girls. I was on cloud nine and went to town to make it as near to perfect for them as I could. It was as though I wanted to make up for the fright we'd all had when it looked as though our family was breaking up for good. Yet again, I was in some way taking the 'blame' for what had happened, even though it was Grant who had cheated. I didn't see it that way at the time though. I just knew I was deliriously happy as the two of us jetted off to Mauritius to see in the New Year, to the same hotel where we had got engaged. We went to the balcony where he had proposed to me and even spoke about renewing our vows later on in the year and having a party to celebrate 'life'. How lucky was I to have such a caring, thoughtful husband?

Back in the UK, he came and watched me take part in *Dancing on Ice* every week until I was eventually voted off. It was such a wonderful, fun time, made all the better because my husband was there supporting me. I obviously hadn't forgotten all the hurt his betrayal had caused me but by then I had definitely gone a long, long way to forgiving him and was truly happy and secure once more. It didn't occur to me that his declarations of remorse and his expressions of love were anything but genuine and I allowed myself to believe his cheating had been a blip, never to be repeated. We were going to grow old together.

Then something began to feel not right again. Grant's pattern of behaviour began to change once more. During the *Dancing on Ice* press machine I'd done an interview about my time on the show and how ecstatic I was to have my marriage back on track. I talked about how happy Grant and I were, how thrilled the girls were to have the family back together and how this time, it was for keeps. But on this occasion he went absolutely ballistic and yet it was such a positive article after the rocky time we'd been through and full of praise for him but he didn't appear to see it that way at all. He actually yelled at me, ranting and raving about discussing our private life, even though it was nothing out of the ordinary. He'd thrown me into this particular drama and this was just a tame 'let's smooth it all over and get back to work' article. I was completely taken aback and just couldn't understand where all this anger had come from. A short while later it emerged that all throughout our reconciliation Grant had kept a foot in both camps. While he was telling me how happy he was, how thrilled we were back together, the other woman was getting a completely different story. When I found out it broke my heart all over again, worse than the first time and there was no going back: second chances yes, but not a third.

From that life-changing moment I finally accepted my husband was never going to be the man he'd promised me he was, to writing this book, I've used every trick in the book to return to the confident, self-assured, happy woman I was. From wine to self-help books, from shrinks to life coaches and good friends, I've tried everything I can to reach a place where I can honestly say I feel healthy and strong once more.

We are all wired differently but if you are thin skinned, sensitive and prone to entering The Prison of Bad Thoughts, I'll help you. I want you to benefit from everything I've discovered along the way and boy, was it a 'journey'. Understanding the bigger picture is crucial and the pattern of behaviour of those around you. A wonderful friend of mine, entrepreneur Richard Farleigh, gave me an astute piece of advice, which you can use in either your business or personal life: 'Why be surprised when the snake bites?' Think about it. The wider you open your mind to human behaviour and patterns the easier it is to deal with not just divorce but any of life's testing situations.

This book isn't about the legal process of divorce although we will touch on it when required, but how you survive it. My divorce from Grant was my second and divorcing in your fifties is totally different from ending a marriage when you're much younger. The second time around you feel you've already made all the mistakes you're ever going to, you are older and wiser and by the time you're ready to commit to someone once again, you're convinced you have it sorted. Maybe that's why I found it all the more painful when I was proved so wrong and found myself facing the world alone again. Also, this time as I discovered, much of the hope and optimism I had in my earlier decades had disappeared and instead I found myself dreading the coming years, fearing I was past my best and had nothing to offer. I'm glad to say I was wrong. I've got plenty to offer and I'm finding new opportunities both in my career and socially. It took me just over three years to come out the other side and reach this point and I promise you so will you.

Taken at a charity ball held at our
dream house in Surrey. Happy days.

Chapter Two
Avoid

Divorce is an excruciatingly difficult road to travel and the longer you have been together, the more entwined your lives are and the worse the journey is. I'm not advocating holding on to painful relationships that are a tangled abuse of power and control, but make sure you both want this, because as I will explain, divorce is going to test you to your emotional and practical limits.

Personally, while I've come to terms with being a divorcee, I can't say I am completely over the trauma and the pain, even though it's been nearly four years now since Grant and I went our separate ways. Don't get me wrong, I'm definitely much stronger and more confident than when I began the journey but I can't pretend I don't have the odd 'down day,' and that what I've been through hasn't taken its toll. It most certainly has. Obviously everyone is different and we all find ourselves embroiled in a split for all manner of personal reasons. But whether you've instigated heading for the divorce courts or been 'forced' into it by your partner; or whether it's something you both agreed you wanted and indeed, it might be the best thing for you in the long-term, I guarantee you will not escape the emotional and/or financial fall-out in some shape or form.

According to the latest available figures from the Office of National Statistics, there were a staggering 111,169 divorces in England and Wales in 2014. Even though this was a drop of 3.1% from the previous year, it's still an extraordinarily high number of people who've decided their marriages aren't worth saving. That's sad.

I'm a great believer in second chances and I honestly feel that knee-jerk reactions have no place in making life-changing decisions. When you're married to someone, it's not just about you; there's a whole network to consider. You've created a life together as a couple and you have immediate family and good friends who are all invested in your marriage and there's the whole business of being a family with joint finances, pension, a home, a mortgage and so on.

Unfortunately when men get their d*** out they often don't think of all these things at the time. How many people are out there who've cheated on their partner and later regret what they did? How many who believed the grass was greener somewhere else when it was just that theirs needed a re-turf or a drop of fertilizer?

Before you go rushing off to see a solicitor, ask yourself: am I doing the right thing? If your partner has cheated on you or behaved badly in some other way, or if you're the one who's played away and think your marriage is doomed, think again. And think carefully. Are you absolutely positive the problems you're facing can't be overcome? Has your other half done something so terrible that it's impossible to forgive and try and rebuild your relationship?

Maybe no one has actually done anything wrong and you've simply fallen out of love with each other? No one ever said marriage is a bed of roses all the time – of course domestic life and routine get boring – but is there any way in which you're able to revive the spark that led you to marry this person in the first place?

I remember reading the results of a survey carried out about a year after I filed for divorce. It showed that about half of divorcees regretted ending their marriages and wished they had tried harder to make them work. In my case, Grant didn't really leave me much choice but ironically, he went on to regret that we divorced. When he appeared on *Celebrity Big Brother* only last year, he told everyone how sorry he was about how much he'd hurt me and how he wished he could turn back the clock.

Apparently, these are divorcees' top ten reasons for regretting their decision:

1. Missing an ex-partner
2. Feeling like a failure
3. Still being in love with an ex-partner
4. Realising they were being unreasonable
5. Feeling lonely
6. Discovering the grass isn't always greener
7. An ex-partner finding someone new
8. Realising they are not better off on their own
9. Damaging the relationship with their children
10. Children's lives being affected

There is absolutely no harm in getting some sound advice from a professional before you make your final decision, before you set into motion a chain of events which will change your life forever. There are many couples counselling services available such as Relate where you can talk through marital issues. If you're in emotional turmoil, wondering if your marriage can possibly survive the problems you're experiencing, you can make an appointment for yourself only and air your worries and concerns in confidence. You may afterwards decide you don't want a divorce at all, but instead you need to find a way to resolve the issues within your marriage.

Or perhaps you and your other half can go together and make an effort to work out your differences. If it doesn't work and divorce is definitely on the cards, then at least you can look back one day and know in your heart you tried your hardest to save your marriage.

Relate

Barbara Honey, Senior Practice Consultant at Relate agrees that it is important to try everything you can to avoid divorce and says the organisation offers a range of services and counselling, not just for adults but for young people and children. 'No matter what stage people are at, they can come and see us and we will try and help them repair the damage,' she states. 'Whether they have just become separated or divorced or are simply thinking about ending a marriage, we'll try and help any member of the family.'

There are Relate Centres across the UK and Wales and funding and client contributions vary. Therefore the cost of a counselling session varies from centre to centre. But please don't let financial worries stop you from making a much-needed appointment as there may be bursary funding available.

Contact details for Relate can be found at the back of this book, including the website which you should look at in the first instance. Anyone is entitled to click on the Live Chat link on the website and speak to a trained counsellor free of charge first before making a face to face appointment.

Relate can also help if your divorce is inevitable, Barbara Honey says, and relationship counsellors are available to help make both sides get through the process as amicably as possible. The service can be particularly useful if there are children involved. 'On-going parental relationship is vital for the well-being of the children and Relate can help ensure their needs are fully met during and after a divorce.'

You might be angry now or feeling that you have no option other than to cut your losses, but you can only make such a momentous decision in the cold light of day. I always think making life-changing moves is like playing chess: think all your moves through. Be calm and be rational when you're weighing everything up because once you opt for divorce and begin the legal process, life will never be the same for either of you again.

Second chances

Most people deserve a second chance – life's not simply black and white. It is possible to forgive if you've been betrayed or hurt in some other way, and by that I don't for a minute mean physically. Abuse is always a no, no.

But in my opinion and from personal experience, I can say that infidelity doesn't necessarily have to be a deal-breaker if the cheater is genuinely sorry and the injured party is able to look past the betrayal. This isn't giving every cheater a hall pass to play away. I'm just saying that there are grey areas and it is possible to stay in the marriage even if one of you has been unfaithful. It obviously needs a huge amount of love, support and understanding on both sides.

After I discovered Grant had been unfaithful to me, somehow we still managed to communicate and I think for us, this was the key to staying together. He was –

eventually — hugely sorry and contrite and I tried my hardest to understand why he did what he did and to make our marriage work. I gave him his second chance because I believed with all my heart we would get through it and build a stronger relationship. Despite what later happened, I don't regret it because I know I did everything in my power to keep our family together and that, to me, meant everything. Whatever happens in life, in a marriage, no one can sit upon a pedestal of righteousness. Statistically, you're unfortunately in the minority if you're lucky enough to have a solid, long-lasting, baggage-free marriage where nothing has ever gone wrong and no mistakes have been made.

About ten months after Grant and I had reconciled and I truly believed his affair with the younger woman was in the past, his behaviour pattern started to change again. First came the uncharacteristic outburst following my interview with a national newspaper talking about how happy we were. That certainly set alarm bells ringing. But this time I was better prepared. As soon as he began changing again, so my suspicions about him grew. Unlike the first time he'd cheated on me the previous year, I refused to give him the benefit of the doubt and this time I immediately began to question if he was seeing the other woman again. My sixth sense told me he was.

Miss Marple

I remember him once saying he was meeting a business contact at Shoreham Airport which in itself was unusual. I went onto his computer but couldn't find any emails confirming the meeting. This was very odd. And when he returned home, I checked the satellite navigation system of his car but couldn't find the location in 'previous destinations' when I knew he would have had to use it to get there. He told me the meeting had gone well and changed the subject, stopping me from asking too many questions.

Grant has always enjoyed cycling but all of a sudden, he began announcing plans to cycle to all sorts of strange places. He has a Garmin device on his bike which plugs into a home computer and logs mileage, yet when I looked, he hadn't been anywhere he claimed to have done. And as our cars were in my name, I had access to the tracker device on each vehicle which again when I checked, told me he was lying about where he was going. I became a regular Miss Marple, logging onto the computer to check journeys he made, credit cards he'd used and text messages he'd sent – iMessage is everywhere. Grant had no idea I could even do these things. As far as he was concerned I was a technophobe, unable to carry out the simplest tasks on a computer. He shouldn't have underestimated me. I hated being the sort of woman who checks up on her husband – I promise you I never, ever used to be – but unfortunately, his behaviour turned me into her.

I remember a friend telling me how she'd suspected her husband of having an affair and secretly swapped her mobile number in his iPhone for the other woman's. So she was exchanging raunchy messages with her own husband for a while and when she got enough ammunition, she confronted him with it. I thought that was quite amusing, although of course it was also the end of their marriage so not very funny after all.

It didn't take me long to collect my own ammunition and sure enough, as I'd suspected, Grant was back seeing the other woman. This time it was even more shocking than the first time I caught him cheating if that's possible because he knew how hard I'd had to dig to forgive him only months earlier. He'd seen my pain and that of the girls and we were only just back on an even keel, or at least I believed we were. But I have to remember he'd also seen Della's pain when he was leaving her for me and he still walked...

To go and hurt me all over again was just mind numbing. This time there were no cries for forgiveness or endless conversations and explanations. He simply said he wanted a different life to the one he had and didn't want to be married any more. And while he did try and come back a few months later I knew in my own heart I had given this marriage all I had and it was time to call it a day. I'd given it my best shot. I tried to put it right and gave him the second chance I believe we all deserve in life. But on his part it was all a big lie. He was in contact with his mistress all along and we were heading for divorce.

Despite this, I still say if you can avoid the divorce courts then please do. Give your marriage and yourself, every chance to succeed because divorce is one of the most painful experiences you will go through; I wouldn't wish it on anyone. But if you know in your heart that you've reached the end of the line with this person and you have no option but to cut them loose, then approach the process with your eyes wide open.

Jayne's story

After fifteen years of marriage, Jayne thought she wanted a divorce from Andy. It was a slow build but it gradually dawned on her that everything about him drove her insane, from the way he munched his food to his insistence on sticking to a routine. She knew exactly what they'd be doing every single weekend – including a quickie on Friday nights – and she was bored rigid.

"I felt like such a bitch because Andy hadn't done anything wrong, he was just so dull," she says. "I wanted some excitement, some spontaneity yet all he wanted was to watch telly every night and have a roast lunch with his parents every Sunday. I knew I couldn't live another fifteen years like that, let alone the rest of my life.

"So even though I knew his family would be devastated and that the children would suffer in the short term, I sat Andy down one evening and told him I had fallen out of love with him and that I wanted a divorce. I blamed myself and through guilt, I said he could have the children fifty per cent of the time."

What Jayne hadn't considered was the ripple effect this decision would have, not just on her and Andy as a couple but on their children, aged eight and ten, her parents, Andy's parents and all their mutual friends. Everyone was shocked and upset and while at the end of the day it was Jayne's choice, she realised she'd be picking up the pieces for a long, long time to come. Not only was she now a single Mum with two miserable, resentful children to care for on her own, but the days they spent with their Dad were incredibly lonely and she found herself missing family life, even though she'd once considered it mundane and dull. Her married friends while still friendly, stopped inviting her to dinner parties so often and she found herself dropped by some acquaintances altogether. Andy, it seemed, was a pretty popular guy and many of their mutual pals took his side after the divorce. What's more, her own parents while attempting to support her, still loved Andy and remained close to him 'for the sake of the grandchildren' so she felt unable to turn to them for sympathy when she was feeling particularly sorry for herself.

"I wish now that I hadn't been in such a hurry to make such a huge decision," she admits. "I should have told Andy exactly how I was feeling and maybe together we could have injected some excitement into our marriage. I wish I'd gone to Relate and spoken to someone about my situation because I know now loads of couples go through bad patches and manage to resolve them. I'm not saying we would necessarily have stayed together because although I did love Andy, I wasn't in love with him anymore. But then again, we might have managed to revive that missing spark and may still be married. The trouble is, I rushed into divorce because I thought it was what I wanted. I wasn't thinking about anyone except myself and I should have tried harder to make it work."

Lucinda's story...

"On our second wedding anniversary, Haydon told me our marriage wasn't 'working out' and he thought we should separate. I was in a state of shock. We'd been together five years before getting married and were trying for a baby. I thought I knew everything about him, yet it turned out he'd been sleeping with an intern at work and while he didn't want to be with her full time, he felt he was too young to be tied down to me. Yet we were both in our early thirties, hardly kids.

I could barely speak all the way home in the car after our 'celebratory' anniversary dinner and he was all sheepish and guilty looking. I wanted to slap him. At least he did the decent thing and moved out that night. He said he wasn't going to her house, but I didn't believe him.

I was sick that night and every morning for a week. I thought it was heartache but it turned out I was pregnant. What a bitter sweet moment when I did the home pregnancy test. Haydon is the first person I would call whenever anything happened, good or bad, but I couldn't tell him he was going to be a Dad, even though I knew he'd be thrilled, despite what he'd done. I felt he didn't deserve to know. By keeping it secret, I was punishing him and having that secret, made me feel a bit more powerful.

Six or seven weeks later, Haydon called me, asking if we could talk. We met in a wine bar near our home in North London, a place we'd visited together dozens of times before. I was upset and nervous as I walked through the door. I thought he was going to ask for a divorce but instead he actually cried, said he'd made a terrible mistake and asked to move back home. I should have said no, that he'd hurt me irretrievably, but I had our baby to consider. Also I was still madly in love with him and I'd been like a zombie for weeks. So I agreed he could move back on the condition that he came to couples counselling with me which he reluctantly agreed to. We had four sessions with a counsellor and it gave me the chance to really vent my hurt and anger at Haydon without him interrupting or making excuses. He was actually pretty shocked at the effect his cheating had had on me and he admitted he'd had his head turned by this attractive woman at work. That really, really hurt.

But the counselling also gave us both the opportunity to admit to each other that in trying for a baby, our love-making had become more of a chore than a pleasure, although that doesn't excuse him straying and looking for passion elsewhere. We agreed to talk out our issues in future and not take the easy way out. It was only weeks later when Haydon moved back home that I told him my news. He was ecstatic and so was I - we were going to be a family.

That was six years ago and we're now proud parents to a five year-old daughter and eighteen month-old twin boys. Haydon is an amazing father. He's grown up a lot and is still sorry for his 'lapse of judgement' as he calls it. I still haven't quite forgiven him for the affair and I will never forget either but I am glad I gave him a second chance. I wouldn't have wanted to be a single parent, although I think I'm strong enough to have managed on my own if I'd had to. What we have now is a wonderful, happy family which is everything I could have dreamed of. I just hope Haydon's truly learned from his mistake and that history won't repeat itself. I've taken that risk and so far, so good."

In a nutshell...

☆ **Don't rush into filing for a divorce** – it will take an emotional and financial toll on you and is not a decision to take lightly.

☆ **Seek advice from friends, family and/or a counsellor** if you are in any doubt whatsoever. There is no harm in taking a step back.

☆ **Are you able to forgive your partner** enough to give him a second chance?

☆ **If there's been physical or emotional abuse,** second chances do not apply.

☆ **The grass looks greener elsewhere** but are you sure it's not possible to revive the missing spark?

☆ **Have you considered the full impact breaking up the family** will have on your children? Decide how you will handle this before setting anything in motion.

☆ **If you've given your relationship every chance** and you know it's definitely over, go into your divorce with your eyes wide open, knowing you've tried everything to make your marriage work.

☆ **If you need to play for time**, do as they say in the north - when in doubt do nowt - don't rush into anything.

I Told You I'd Move On

I told you I'd let you go someday. Honestly it was the hardest thing I've ever done but it was worth it. For me, for my heart.

You hurt me so bad. You killed my trust, you changed me.

I knew I could be strong enough to let you go. I knew it and I did it. I can't explain how proud I am. Because I'm the only one who knows how much you hurt me.

— Anonymous

Chapter Three
The Die Is Cast

So, you've done everything in your power to make your marriage work. You've compromised, forgiven and forgotten, turned a blind eye, changed your mind time and time again, sought advice, promised to change, extracted promises from your other half, thought about the effect on your children, on your life together, your extended family and group of friends...Despite endless counselling from loved ones and perhaps even from the professionals plus a great deal of wine-drinking, tears and soul searching, you've come to the conclusion that you have no other choice but to seek a divorce.

It's an indescribably painful position to be in and you'll be reeling with misery as you contemplate what lies ahead. But burying your head in the sand and hoping it will all go away is not the answer. You owe it to yourself and your children if you have any, to take some sort of control and carve out the best possible deal for everyone involved in this whole sorry mess.

Of course I'm coming at this from my own point of view in that I didn't want to get a divorce but felt I had no choice after I discovered Grant had cheated on me, not once but twice. But perhaps you're the one who's met someone else and wants out of your marriage? Or maybe you're just not in love anymore and know divorce is the best option for you both. Then again, you might be in my position – 'forced' into a divorce you don't really, truly want – but knowing for the sake of your sanity, self-worth and future happiness, you have to free yourself once and for all from your partner.

In truth you need to have achieved Chapter Six to deal

best with this chapter but unfortunately if you don't get this bit right and instead sink into a crate of wine, tears, anger, pain and maybe a one night stand, the process will be longer and even harder than it's going to be. Don't let that happen to you because as I've discovered myself, whatever position you're coming from to reach this point in your life, there is a whole world waiting for you to go out and join it again.

If you are the one filing for divorce, this is serious business and time for you to be practical. You will require legal guidance and help because let me tell you, disentangling yourself from your spouse, can be an absolute minefield. There are so many issues to consider and not just financial ones. For instance, when you go your separate ways, who do the children live with? Who makes life-impacting decisions for them if they live with you? What if their Dad wants them and fights for custody? If you've committed adultery, are you fearful it could affect your rights to the care of your children or to your share of the family's finances?

I'm not legally qualified to answer all of these questions. Instead I've turned to the experts here and I'm grateful to them for offering their knowledge. But having gone through the process, I can tell you that I know the importance of finding a good solicitor and how vital it is to be massively pro-active yourself. Don't simply pick a solicitor at random. This person is going to be vitally important to you for many months – or even years – and needs to be both qualified and understanding. I'm not suggesting you use your solicitor as a counsellor; it's not their role to talk you through the emotional ups and downs of your divorce – and a qualified counsellor would be less expensive – but they will need to know the most intimate, private details of your relationship so you must be confident and secure enough in this person to be able to bare your soul and trust them to get you the best deal possible.

Invest

Tracey Rodford who is a specialist Family Solicitor, working in a Central London practice, says 'Invest in your divorce for the best possible outcome. It will be worth it in the long run, no matter what your view of lawyers may be in the beginning. Lawyers do not seek to capitalise on your misfortune; I like to think they fight for equality and justice.

'One party tends to know more about the family finances than the other. Quite often (although not always) the woman is at home, raising the children while the husband is the bread winner and knows about the financial side of things. When it comes to divorce, my job is to ensure the assets are fairly distributed, even though one party may believe they are entitled to more because they're the money earner. This is not the case.'

Knowledge is power so do your research and have a clear understanding of everything you're up against, in particular your financial situation. Too many people use up their solicitor's — very costly — time which is money from the 'pot', all the while bemoaning the philandering sins of their cheating partner. Your ex-to-be has cost you enough already so don't let them cost you a penny more.

I wasn't prepared at all initially and arrived at my lawyer's office for the first time, with nothing but tears and my own sob story. It was only when she began asking me questions such as who owned what, how much money was in which accounts, how much was left on the mortgage and so on, that I quickly realised I didn't know as much about the Bovey family finances as I should have. It didn't take me long to learn and I methodically set about putting together a file of documents covering everything from our weekly grocery and petrol bills to the interest on our mortgage statements. My step-daughter Claudia even set up an Excel spreadsheet for me and I began to enter every single item I spent money on. It was an important learning curve for me, as it will be for you; your financial 'pot' is more than likely going to be slashed in half once your divorce comes through and it's vital you understand exactly what your money is spent on in order to go forward alone and what your budget is likely to be from now on.

That July 2013 day I arrived at my lawyer's for a showdown meeting with my soon-to-be-ex and his solicitor, I may still have had a lot of tears for the situation in which I'd found myself but I also had a solid financial record and was thoroughly prepared for what was to come. So when the meeting between me,

Grant and our solicitors began, I was able to negotiate our financial settlement from a position of confidence with my new-found knowledge.

It might sound a little unnecessary but you truly need to list everything you spend before you see your lawyer. It will save you both valuable time and money. When I say everything, I mean everything: groceries, toiletries, petrol, travel, children's clothing, party gifts, teachers' presents, tutoring, music or dance lessons, stamps, Christmas pressies, utility bills, you name it. It's a time-consuming task but once it's done, you'll have a record to refer to over and over again. It's imperative you don't miss out anything because this could be the key to your future financial security. If you are going to be seeking a certain amount to live on, you will be required to demonstrate how much it is you actually do need, in order to support yourself and the children. As long as the money is there and this is what you're used to spending, the chances are it will be reflected in your divorce settlement. You must be as frank and honest with your lawyer as possible. There's no point in claiming you regularly spend £1,000 a month on flowers if your joint monthly income is a fraction of this amount. And by the same token, don't fail to include items you might not consider imperative, such as your monthly gym membership for instance. If you've been going to the gym for years and the money to pay for it is there, why shouldn't you be able to continue? Keeping fit and healthy is good for everyone and will help you to deal with a lot of the s*** life throws at you. In my experience, anything considered 'reasonable' is acceptable when both sides are attempting to reach a fair settlement.

Be realistic

Now we've all heard about 'grasping' women who take their poor, hard done by husbands to the 'cleaners', leaving him virtually penniless in a damp bedsit while they retain the cosy family home, car, children and pet dog. I'm sure there have been cases like that in the past and I do vaguely recall a time when judges appeared to come down in favour of the wife, awarding her the marital home and custody of the children, seemingly at the expense of the husband. But it's not like that anymore and if you think you're going to be allowed to stay in your home while turfing your cheating husband out on the street, it may not happen like that. Both parties are entitled to have enough money to be able to support themselves post-divorce and often it means that the standard of living for both is significantly reduced. After all, any assets have been carved up and what formerly propped up just one household now has to support two.

There was a time when a woman who'd spent a large chunk of her life out of the workplace, raising the children and running the home, could expect to be taken care of after divorce. (And vice versa of course as there are plenty of house husbands.) Again, that is not so much the case anymore. The market place has changed and attitudes have shifted and judges – if the divorce gets as far as the courtroom – often expect women to go out and find a job, even if it is poorly paid and deemed low or un-skilled. Even though this seems incredibly unfair if you've got little to show on your CV other than full-time housewife and mother, it is fast becoming a fact of life.

A court may award you half or little more, of your joint assets and something towards the care of the children, but you may not receive maintenance for yourself. Your ex's lawyer will see to it that he too has enough to live on, makes a contribution towards the care of his children and that's more or less it – unless he happens to be wealthy in which case he may choose to be more generous or ordered to be.

Do you remember the case of a former supermodel who received a settlement of a mere £58m in cash plus assets of £25m? Her husband was allegedly worth twice as much and she claimed she was used to the lifestyle they'd shared – including four bottles of face cream at cost of £9,400! – and therefore deserved a healthy payout when he divorced her. As outrageous as this may sound, she was entitled to the obscene sums because it's true, it is what she was used to and the money was there. And no, she probably didn't need to rush out and get a job waiting tables to supplement her income.

Sadly, for most people the sums involved in divorce settlements are far less so be prepared to have to alter your lifestyle. If you've not had to think about working for many years, you're bound to find the prospect of resurrecting some sort of career extremely daunting. Not only are you a single woman again, perhaps a single Mum, you're also having to support yourself and rejoin the workforce. Remember, if you can successfully run a household and raise a family, you already have a damn good skill set for all number of jobs, so don't underestimate yourself. It may not be easy to begin with but unless you're past retirement age or physically incapacitated, it will be possible for you to find employment again. What's more, you may grow to enjoy your new-found independence and hopefully acquire a whole new set of friends and acquaintances.

Tips from a divorce lawyer:

Not all divorces need to conclude in a legal battle and good, early legal advice can help to avoid highly contentious litigation and large legal fees.

Although there are no short cuts or quick solutions when divorcing, depending on the dynamics of your relationship, there are options that can make the process less stressful and expensive. There are also some simple things that you can do to assist those who are advising you and get to the reality of the financial situation and a settlement more efficiently:

1. Be prepared – do your homework and know about your finances.

2. Don't be unrealistic – you have to accept that life and your financial position change on divorce.

3. Don't use the children as a weapon – consider how the breakdown of your marriage will affect them. Try and agree contact arrangements for them with your ex.

4. The divorce and financial settlement are not the same thing – the process of resolution of

matrimonial finances is separate to the legal divorce and although your lawyer will advise you to do the two in conjunction one can be done independently of the other.

5. Settling matrimonial finances is where most couples fall into difficulty. The best and most effective approach to resolving finances, with or without professional support, is to approach disclosure as honestly and openly as possible.

6. Mediation – if you and your ex are able to manage to discuss matters and can work together with the benefit of a professional to resolve matters, mediation may be an option to consider. However, mediation will only work if there is a level of equality between you and your ex.

7. The court process – if you reach the position where you are instructing lawyers, it does not mean that you will end up in court. There are non-contentious ways in which your lawyers can operate to resolve matters for you as efficiently as possible. If however this fails and matters cannot be resolved, the next stage is to commence court proceedings.

Uncontested divorce flowchart

1. Send Divorce Petition to local Family Court

2. Copy of Petition sent to your spouse

5 Grounds for Divorce
Adultery
Unreasonable behaviour
Desertion
Two years separation (consent required)
Five years separation (no consent required)

3. Your spouse completes and returns an Acknowledgement of Service Form

4. If undefended, you complete a statement in support of a Petition and Application for Decree Nisi

5. Court considers all papers and confirms your marriage has irretrievably broken down

6. Date is set for Decree Nisi

7. You can apply for Decree Absolute 6 weeks and 1 day after Decree Nisi

Decree Absolute.
You are divorced but financial ties between you and your spouse are not automatically cut.

Sunita's story...

"When my husband Raj decided I was surplus to his requirements and said he wanted a divorce, I was not just broken-hearted, I was scared what the future held for me and the kids. Up until then, we'd enjoyed a comfortable lifestyle: Raj worked as an IT specialist for a medium-sized company in Bristol while I'd given up my job as a beautician twelve years earlier when our eldest daughter was born. I always thought I'd return to work at some point but we went on to have two more girls and my life was pretty full raising three daughters, looking after Raj and running our home. We were both happy in our roles – at least I thought we were.

My parents and Raj's were furious with him. He'd met a single mum at the gym he went to each morning and said he hadn't meant to fall in love with her but he had. Bastard. My Dad helped me find a highly-recommended, tough-talking solicitor who promised she'd help me get a good divorce settlement. I'll always be grateful to her for helping me through some of the worse months of my life. But she also made it clear that I had little chance of remaining in the family home because as she explained, Raj would also need somewhere to live after the split. He wanted shared custody of the girls so it was only fair they had somewhere to stay when they were with him. In my opinion there was nothing fair about it at all. He was the one who destroyed our happiness so why the hell did I have to give up the beautiful home I'd poured love into for the best part of fifteen years? But as my solicitor tactfully pointed out, I was still in my forties – not old by any means – and perfectly capable of getting a job to support myself in the future. It was a wake-up call.

My days of keeping house and collecting the girls from school, rustling up healthy meals and not having to worry about paying the bills was over. I had to rejoin the workplace and start contributing financially to the family.

Three years on and I'm in a much better place. I have a part-time position in a beauty salon and thanks to my boss, I've received training to update my skills. Raj has the children every other weekend so I have some time to myself and yes, I am seeing a new man although it's still early days.

I received a little over fifty per cent of the proceeds of the house sale and managed to buy a cottage just outside Bristol, outright. It's smaller than we were used to but we're all settled now and content. It finally feels like 'home'.

I get no spousal maintenance from my ex, just a fixed amount for the girls but I will receive half of his pension when the time comes (thanks to my solicitor's insistence) and as I'm the girls' primary carer, I receive some child benefit and working tax credits so I can pay the bills. When the girls are a bit older, I intend going back to work full-time so hopefully I can stop claiming benefits."

The pactical stuff

Actually filing for divorce or being at the receiving end of a divorce petition can be a daunting prospect. How complex it all becomes will depend on the amount of money involved and whether or not you have children. And of course, the reasons why the divorce is necessary may also come into play.

Here, Anne-Lise Wall, a Senior Mediator and Family and Collaborative Lawyer with Morrisons Solicitors LLP has generously agreed to contribute to this book by personally answering some frequently asked questions:

What is the cheapest way to obtain a divorce? What if you have no money?
The cheapest way to obtain a divorce is DIY. The forms are available online or from your local Family County Court. If you have no money (i.e. you are on low-income or benefits) you can apply to be exempt from paying the £550 fee by completing a form which is available from the court. You have to put down all your outgoings and income and the court will decide if you can have exemption from paying the court fees.

What difference does having children make, if any?
Having children makes no difference to obtaining a divorce.

Can you divorce online?

As stated above, the forms are available online, but once completed they need to be posted to the Family Court with responsibility for dealing with divorce for your area. After lodging the Divorce Petition, it is possible to correspond with the court by email.

What if my other half doesn't want a divorce?

There are two grounds for divorce where the co-operation of your other half is needed: adultery (where they need to answer 'yes' to the question on the Acknowledgement of Service form, 'do you admit the adultery alleged?') and where they need to consent to a petition on the grounds of two years separation. If any of the other three grounds for divorce are used, ('behaviour', five years separation and desertion) the other spouse does not have to agree. They could defend a petition but in practice, less than one per cent of all divorces end up as contested cases.

What if I don't want a divorce but my other half does?

I would personally suggest marriage counselling such as Relate. (See chapter two.) Otherwise see the above.

Is there any benefit for one person filing as opposed to being served papers?

Generally the answer is 'no'. However, in the very rare cases where the petition details allegations of extreme 'behaviour' which the petitioner intends to rely on in the financial proceedings, there would be a benefit in being the petitioner. The other reason is more practical. If there is a reason to think that your spouse might drag their heels, and you want to get on with the divorce, you might be better to start the proceedings by issuing the petition. Alternatively, you might want your other half to start so that they pay for it, as the petitioner is required to pay the fee.

How long does the process take?
Usually around six to twelve months although some courts are currently experiencing delays.

In your experience, what effect does divorce have on children?
This is a huge topic! There have been numerous research studies looking into this and in brief, the results have shown that divorce can have a detrimental effect on the children. They can experience grief, loss, anger, shame and often blame themselves for the split. It can affect their behaviour, so that some children regress, some become aggressive at school, attention spans can shorten, sleep and eating patterns can be affected. However, in my experience, when parents manage their separation well and both tell the children together that they intend to separate, but that they will always continue to love them, this can help the children adjust.

How do you decide who the children live with?
The decision about who the children are to live with really depends on practical issues such as accommodation and

caring for the children. It is more usual now for parents to share care of the children. This doesn't always mean that they spend fifty per cent of the week with one parent and fifty per cent with the other. Ideally, the decision is taken by the parents after considering what is best for the children. If they are unable to manage having a reasonable discussion about this, they could attend mediation to try and resolve the issues. If there is serious conflict, an application can be made to ask the court to decide.

Is mediation compulsory?

a) No mediation is not compulsory. If someone wants to start court proceedings for financial orders in divorce or about children, they have to attend a MIAMS (Mediation Information and Assessment Meeting) session with a mediator.

b) At the end of a mediation process, the mediator prepares two summaries: one setting out the finances and one called a Memorandum of Understanding, setting out what the couple propose. (This is a 'Without Prejudice' document.) Both summaries are then handed to the family lawyers to prepare the court order(s) based on the information in the summaries. It is the court order which is binding.

c) Mediation costs vary. Some mediators offer legal aid.

d) Mediation is voluntary and both parties need to attend.

Sometimes (though rarely) the court can order that parties attend mediation.

e) MIAMS meetings take place with a mediator who assesses whether the case is suitable for mediation and provides information about the various process options. In the event that mediation is not appropriate or suitable, the mediator will sign the relevant page of the application form so that the person can make the court application either for children's cases or for financial orders in divorce.

Mediation

Wirral-based Donna Goodwin trained as a mediator and set up her own successful practice, 1st For Mediation. Donna recognises that going to court sometimes is a daunting experience – solicitors and barristers for both parties are there to try and get the best for their clients. She believes this is where mediation can be an option worth considering, to make sure both sides are happy with the outcome.

'A mediator is an independent and neutral negotiator, who is able to talk to both sides and who works for the benefit of the "whole family", Donna explains. 'As there is just one mediator, he or she will have a clear idea of the feelings, wishes, hopes and fears of both parties. The mediator is working with the interests of both parties in mind.

'To protect themselves, most couples turn to solicitors in the hope of getting as good a deal as they can. Solicitors are not allowed to act for both sides, as they are obliged to act in their client's best interests. Therefore, each separating couple has to use two separate sets of lawyers, and the bills can soon mount up. This is at a time when the income and wealth of one household has to be stretched to provide for two.

'With mediation, as there are not two lawyers sending demanding letters to each other, the process can be quicker and less expensive. It is particularly important where children are involved, because the parents will have a continuing relationship for as long as they both are providing parental care.

'The mediator will gather all the relevant financial information and, by using his or her knowledge and negotiating skills, try to draw the two sides together into a sensible, fair and practical agreement that will be acceptable to both of them.

'This may mean moving them from their entrenched positions (typically "She's not getting her hands on my salary" and "If he thinks I'm going to move out of this house, he can think again") to whatever solution is in the best interests of the family.

'Mediation is about achieving a situation where no one loses, preventing either party "losing face".'

Donna says that there are three difficult issues that family mediators may need to discuss with clients:

1. Finances

In a divorce or separation the income into the former family home will most likely change, sometimes dramatically, particularly if for example a father leaves and he is the main wage earner, while the mother might have a part-time job only or be the full-time carer of the children. The father may believe he can no longer afford to cover the family's financial needs as he now has to pay for a separate roof over his own head and another set of bills etc. There may be confusion as to who pays what, due to joint liabilities such as the children's expenses. The mediator has to look at the situation from both sides so that each party can afford to sustain their new lives going forward.

2. Access

With a divorce or separation, communication has usually broken down between both parents therefore making access arrangements difficult. The children's welfare has to be put first and the need to establish time spent with both parents for the children is very important. It could be that if one parent has had an affair and may still be in a relationship with the other person, this can cause a lot of issues and emotional distress between parties as to what is appropriate and each will be thinking of their own needs. It could be that one parent has moved much further away, so more consideration is needed around travelling, days spent together rather than hours and around school life so attendance is not affected. Birthdays, Christmas and in-law arrangements all need to be considered.

3. Property

With a divorce or separation, both parties will need to decide who will live where. Can one of them stay in the same house or will you sell up and both move? Who will get what from the home and where will pets live? Running two homes inevitably means surviving on less income. There may be no equity in the marital home or they may not own their own home. This will all place financial pressure on the family. Both parties will also have an emotional attachment to the family home which could cause them to choose or prioritise in a certain way. Consideration needs to be given to the children living in the home, location of schooling, and affordability of the main carer to move or stay at the home till the youngest child has left full time education and how this would affect the other parent.

"Quite frankly, going to mediation was a waste of time for me and my ex. We paid for six sessions which consisted of us airing our grievances before reaching some sort of tentative agreement. Afterwards my ex would completely renege on everything and we'd go back to square one the following week. He just refused to take the process seriously and because what we agreed on wasn't legally binding, he knew he could go back on his word. Unfortunately, that's just the kind of individual he is. In the end, even the mediator said we were getting nowhere and suggested the only option was to let our solicitors thrash it out which they did, at great expense to us both".

Katrin, 49.

Susan's story...

"When Gary and I split up, we thought we were mature and rational enough to organise our own divorce without paying for costly solicitors. We were in loads of debt which is one of the reasons our marriage broke down and we both wanted to get a clean break as quickly as possible.

I downloaded the relevant paperwork and we filed it with our local Family Court in Croydon. But when we went to the initial hearing, it soon became obvious there were some things we didn't agree on such as how much of Gary's pension I was entitled to (I wanted half as I'd always looked after the children while he worked full-time) and how much access he should have. The judge told us to go to mediation which was frustrating as the idea had been to speed things up but it wasn't up for discussion. I was also worried about the cost implications but we managed to agree a fixed fee for three one-hour sessions with a local firm of mediators.

The mediator was a very calm, experienced middle-aged man who just listened to us both and made a lot of notes. He asked questions but didn't really give his own opinions. We each got a chance to voice our positions and after three sessions, we did manage to reach a settlement which we were both content with. The mediator drew up our joint statement which we both signed and it was sent to the Family Court. After that, it was more or less a case of rubber stamping the paperwork and our decree nisi came through about six weeks later.

In hindsight, if I'd had the money I would have gone to mediation first but also engaged a solicitor to fight for a better deal for me. But we did what we could afford to do at the time and the main thing is our divorce went through with as little acrimony as possible."

Fiona's story...

"My journey through divorce and once being a family has been a difficult road. I was with my ex-husband for just over twenty years, we did so much together in life, sharing dreams with our careers and having two beautiful children We got married in 1999. We always knew what each other wanted and were always happy to please each other along the way.

The strain in our relationship came when we both had careers and two children, with our lives being so busy we seemed to drift apart. The final reason we separated doesn't matter here for the purposes of this book but what I want to focus on is what happened to our family and marriage as a result of the legal system.

From being a Mum and wife I was thrust into a world of legal paperwork and advice from solicitors which was all above me at the time. I was so emotional and stressed that I wasn't thinking straight at all, I had no one to advise me correctly in my family and I had lost my best friend which was my husband, so this allowed the legal system to take over.

When we went to court I realised through the barristers that it's a big competition and they make you feel as if it's a win or lose situation. So if you don't get what they think you should be getting, you've lost everything which isn't really true. What's really important is your life outside the court room, not a legal order or some piece of paper. And in the middle of it all are the children, these little people who are being pushed around by the system. My children didn't really know what was going on, they love both of us.

One thing I knew was that even though I didn't want to be with my ex-husband in a relationship, I didn't want them to not see their Dad. It's important that children have access to both parents. It's not the children's fault that you have separated.

The legal system cut off all contact between me and my ex-husband; nothing could be discussed amicably between us. We didn't get the chance to see if what the court decided was what we both wanted too.

It has taken our family around five years to come out of the effects of the divorce, there is so much to deal with, if planning your separation falls apart and too many professionals get involved before you know what is happening, it can have an effect right through the family, including grandparents.

When you have children you are together with them until they are into adulthood and beyond, birthdays; Christmas; getting married; birth of their children and so on - the parental link is never broken. So it is massively important to try and separate amicably no matter what the reasons are - you all have a life and a future in front of you.

I believe had my marriage gone through mediation the outcome could have been so different. I would recommend trying Family Mediation first."

In a nutshell...

☆ **Invest in your divorce** for the best possible outcome, especially if there are finances and children involved.

☆ **Don't pick a solicitor at random**, do your research. See at least three before making your choice.

☆ **Get financially savvy.** Make sure you know everything there is about your income and outgoings before your first solicitor's appointment. It will save you money in the long run.

☆ **You can manage your own divorce** if you and your partner are splitting amicably – it's cheaper and can be quicker than costly solicitors. But if there's a lot of money at stake, if there are children involved or if there's abuse or friction in the relationship, this is not always advisable.

☆ **Be realistic:** you may not be able to live the lifestyle you're used to once your divorce is finalised. Be prepared to return to the workplace if necessary.

☆ **Mediation is not compulsory** but is advised for determining financial settlements, and especially when there are children to take into consideration. It is a paid-for service, however some firms offer legal aid.

☆ **Mediators are an agnostic third-party** who listen to both sides before preparing two documents for each party's lawyers: one setting out the finances and one called Memorandum of Understanding, setting out what the couple propose. This information is not legally binding until a court order is prepared and granted.

☆ **Mediation can help to achieve a fair settlement** for both parties. Mediators will gather information on finances, access to the children and who will live where.

☆ **With mediation,** the route to divorce can often be quicker and cheaper, as your lawyer will be presented with all the relevant information for your desired outcome and can therefore act accordingly and in your best interests.

"Daily I walk around my small, picturesque town with a thought bubble over my head: 'Person Going Through A Divorce.' When I look at other people, I automatically form thought bubbles over their heads. 'Happy Couple With Stroller', 'Innocent Teenage Girl With Her Whole Life Ahead Of Her' . . . 'Young Kids Kissing Publicly.' Then every so often I see one like me, one of the shambling gaunt women without makeup, looking older than she is: 'Divorcing Woman Wondering How The Fuck This Happened.'"

– Suzanne Finnamore,
Split: A Memoir of Divorce

Chapter Four
Grief

Every counsellor I've ever spoken to, every book I've ever read has had to admit the galling fact that death is actually easier to reconcile with than divorce, for two main reasons: it's final and there has been no rejection.

After fifteen mainly happy years together, from the age of thirty-eight to fifty-three, Grant and I were divorced and I was utterly bereft. How had it come to this? We were massively connected – our lives together spanned from 1998 to 2013 – and I had learned to be step-mum to three fabulous kids, now three fabulous young women, whom I love very much. We'd been through the trauma of many unsuccessful IVF attempts, three house moves, working together, holidays, weddings and the integration of every part of our lives with family and friends who loved us both. No wonder breaking-up left me feeling as if someone had died.

The grief of a divorce is very real and, just as with a bereavement, you have to expect it. Feelings of grief are inevitable and actually healthy even though it doesn't feel like it at the time. Allow all the natural emotions to take their course, deal with them and come to terms with your loss. The eventual goal is to actually get over the trauma of your divorce and find happiness again but that's some way off, I know.

"Grief is the emotional contract of divorce."
– Cheryl Nielsen

If you're anything like I was in the early days after my marriage ended, you're probably experiencing feelings of despair, anxiety and deep sadness. Even if you've reached this point through choice, facing the future alone after sharing your life and your dreams with another person for however many years is desperately sad, miserable, daunting, terrifying, bewildering and lonely. You may well be asking yourself why you allowed yourself to get here, why didn't you work harder to save your marriage? What if you'd been a better wife? What if you'd compromised more? Forgiven more? Been kinder, smarter, more attentive?

As I tried to explain in Chapter Two, some of these are the sort of questions you need to ask yourself before filing for divorce and maybe you did. Yet here you are. Remember, you've set out on the road to divorce for good reasons and now your journey is underway, it's not going to be a smooth path but one way or another you will reach the other side.

This might sound like an understatement but you're not going to feel better overnight. Grief is a very personal emotion and everyone copes with it differently. So go ahead and cry, scream, shout and switch off from the world. I know I did. I was totally alone and had no one to think about but myself and I'm not ashamed to admit I did wallow for a time.

We're all entitled to have a selection of 'duvet days', totally pissed off days when all we want to do is howl at the unfairness of it all. But ultimately — and I say this from experience — they'll not improve your situation. I remember when I was having a full-on snotty, snivelling day and my Mum rang to check up on me. We had the conversation about how horrid I was feeling and how I was struggling to achieve anything. Mum asked, 'What do you look like?' and I replied, 'Awful'. She told me in no uncertain terms: 'Well go and have a shower, blow-dry your hair, put on your face and call me back.' I meekly followed her instructions. It was like putting on my armour, ready to do business and attack life from the front instead of lying like a foetal ball on the floor. By the time I rang Mum back I have to be honest, I did feel a lot better.

If you have children though, their feelings have to come first. You'll need to reassure them that life isn't going to change for the worse — even though this may not be the case. For now they need to hear their little worlds aren't going to be turned upside down any more than absolutely necessary. Their well-being is always going to be your priority, more so now than ever. But if you can take some time for yourself to come to terms with the loss of your marriage by calling in favours from family and friends who can babysit or invite them over for playdates, then it's important to do just that. Struggling to hold it together in front of others, especially little children who look to you for strength, is a Herculean task and I guarantee you'll feel better if you can let it all out in privacy once in a while.

Here I'd like to introduce you to Dr Karen Finn, a very wise and experienced Divorce Coach who has helped literally thousands of women through the pain of their marriage break-up. She can explain the raw emotions of grief and loneliness associated with divorce much better than I can and hopefully you'll take some comfort from her words because what you're going through right now, is natural and to be expected and you're not alone:

Although divorce isn't the death of a living being, it is absolutely the passing of a way of life. And as with any demise, there is a grief process that begins the moment the journey of divorce begins.

For some their journey of divorce begins long before they ever tell their spouse they no longer want to be married. These people are grieving during their marriage – sometimes for years – before they're able to admit to their partner that they're through.

For others their bereavement begins when their spouse announces that their marriage is over. It's a shock that often throws them into a state of denial and disbelief and even yearning for an understandable closure like the death of their former spouse.

Mourning isn't what anyone really expects when their (or someone else's) marriage ends. We've all been taught to anticipate anger and maybe even hating our ex, but to experience such sadness and pain that at times you wonder if it's worth continuing on is beyond our imagination. And yet that's what many people experience when they divorce – a grief so deep that they have difficulty getting out of bed in the morning, sleeping at night, or simply taking care of themselves.

Because a period of bereavement is largely unanticipated with divorce, when you go through yours you might wonder if you've lost your mind. Your thoughts and emotions will be so unfamiliar and not fit with what you think divorce should be like that it's normal to fear that your sanity disappeared along with everything else.

The mental and emotional kaleidoscope of grappling with divorce is terrifying until you understand what it is. Your mind is a problem-solving machine. When you divorce and experience the deep pain of loss, your brain goes into over-drive trying to figure out a solution so the pain will stop. It doesn't stop at the acceptable solutions, it throws everything possible up as a potential solution for you to cull through.

Under normal conditions, you easily deal with this popcorn effect of ideas to solve your problems and toss out the "crazy" ones.

Unfortunately, divorce isn't a normal circumstance. You're operating at much less than ideal because you've lost your appetite, you're having difficulty sleeping, you're dealing with a legal system that is completely unfamiliar, and you're feeling utterly alone. So, when you start having thoughts that are totally unlike you as you deal with your divorce, they loom large in your imagination and you begin worrying that there's something seriously wrong with you. (So long as you don't plan to act on any of the inappropriate thoughts you're having, you're fine. But if you start to consider them even remotely appropriate, it's time to immediately seek help.)

Divorce is not a normal situation. It's not something that you planned for on your wedding day. But by understanding what to expect when you divorce, you'll be better able to make your way through the sadness and pain.

Initially, divorce is all about loss. You lose things, beliefs, experiences, and dreams that deserve mourning because you've lost precious pieces of your life. Allowing yourself to experience the grief and slowly begin to realise that your life must and will go on with different things, altered beliefs, new experiences and dreams is how you will make it through the bereavement of divorce.

Dr Karen Finn

Loneliness

Unless you've experienced emotional loneliness it's difficult to explain but from your throat to your solar plexus you feel paralysed by emotion.

From the day I was born I had never been on my own. I am part of a close, Midlands family who nurtured my childlike needs then supported me in everything I did. Although I didn't have many boyfriends – more about that later – I realise I was never actually alone and without a partner until the end of my marriage to Grant. If you spend any time studying the subject of human behaviour as I have done, you'll learn that we are pack animals by nature. Moments of isolation are often required to think and process but generally, we seek out others; we are team players. We hunt in packs, we like to belong; we're territorial about our homes, country and beliefs. To procreate we need a mate of the opposite sex and to bring up our children, we prefer to do it as a couple, nurturing them together. So when we suddenly find ourselves alone – not through choice – it can be isolating, incredibly lonely and very frightening. I spent some time studying anthropology when I found myself in this position. It's truly fascinating and I would encourage you to do the same.

For the first time in many years I found myself alone with no one else to answer to, no one to question me, run anything by, agree or disagree with me or have to please. Maybe you can breathe a sigh of relief and relish this new-found freedom. If so, I'm pleased for you. But maybe like me, you're simply sad, lonely and wondering what the hell you do now.

"Loneliness is a normal yet incredibly uncomfortable part of divorce. Somehow everyone else (maybe even your ex) continues to move forward instead of stopping or at least slowing down to truly mourn the passing of your marriage with you. You come to realise that in some strange way your divorce has made you separate and different from the rest of the world – at least the married world that you used to feel part of. This realisation adds to the mountain of misery you're already experiencing."

Dr Karen Finn

Fucking Christmas!

I did everything I could to deal with my own brand of loneliness, from seeing friends even when I wasn't in the mood to socialise, to accepting work commitments which normally I wouldn't have felt the need to accept. For instance, the first December after our divorce, I was offered the chance to take part in Channel 4's *The Jump* and I didn't hesitate in accepting; it saved my soul. Getting a divorce changed everything for me when it came to Christmas which is normally my favourite time of the year. I was no longer in the same house, the decorations were in storage, it seemed pointless getting a tree and there was no one to cook Christmas lunch for. I know if you've got children this isn't necessarily the case, you have to make it a special day for them. But there will be Christmases when they're with their Dad and you find yourself alone or invited to spend the day with other family members or friends. Wherever you find yourself, especially that first festive season after you've split up, you're likely to be extremely sad and a little lonely. You'll feel as if you're surrounded by couples playing happy families, a cuckoo in everyone else's nest. It's a harsh reminder of how much your life has changed.

I flew to Innsbruck to train for *The Jump*, hurling myself down that ridiculous shoot into the air. It was the most frightening thing I'd ever done but in my fear I felt strangely comfortable and alive again and the concentration required took my mind away from my troubles. I didn't really talk

The Jump - so grateful to this show
for getting me through my first
Christmas.

to anyone about what was going on, I just plastered on a smile and concentrated hard on learning a new skill. It was a wonderful and much-needed distraction. When I returned to the UK a week before Christmas, I held on to the fact that I'd be going back to Austria for six weeks. All I had to do was get through the week...

The whole Christmas and New Year period was just excruciating. I spent Christmas Eve at Sally's Meen's house. The three girls were with me for the first part then went off to stay with their Dad. Sally's brother-in-law Paul Keating and I, who were both in the same situation, enthusiastically drank our way into Christmas Day putting the world to rights as only two inebriated people can. I remember waking up to my excited Goddaughter Tilly and her sister Flora at 6am desperate to take me downstairs and see if Santa had been. My head was banging: I'd turned into the Grinch.

On New Year's Eve I watched the fireworks on Lambeth Bridge and went through the motions but I wasn't really there, too soon, too raw to enjoy the festive season. At that time of year you're constantly reminded that this is family time, when you share your good fortune with your loved ones, just being together in one big happy bubble. I know I still had much to be thankful for, there's always someone worse off etc, etc. But when you're at your lowest ebb, experiencing grief it's difficult to feel anything other than your own selfish emotions. Not only do you feel not in the mood to celebrate, but everyone is looking forward to the New Year and all you can think about is: 'What will the New Year bring?' I remember feeling terrified of the future, even though I was desperate to see the back of 2013.

Until this year when the summer was over, I started to feel physically sick. It's hard to explain but while everyone else is looking forward to Halloween and Bonfire Night, all I could think about was that the big one was nearly there – Christmas – and I started to panic. I used to absolutely love Christmas, everything about it made me feel warm and fuzzy inside, from the excitement of present shopping, to decorating the tree and the house in glittering, twinkling ornaments. I used to adore doing everything for the girls at this magical time of year, nothing was too much trouble, Every present had to be beautifully wrapped and by Christmas Eve, everything was prepared to perfection. Remember, this is the woman who wrote the book *Perfect Christmas* and it came straight from the heart.

Even as I write, my eyes are filling up with tears because although I'm through my divorce now and see a bright future ahead, I remember how lonely and scared I felt that first December. Even last Christmas while I was in the throes of writing this book, I signed up to do a panto with no other reason than distraction. With rehearsals and two performances a day, it meant I had only Christmas Day off and the rest of the time I was preoccupied with the show. I'd rather have been in my own home, cooking a delicious lunch for my family but I knew I had to accept that's my past and I'm very fortunate to be offered the opportunities which come my way.

In the lonely, early post-divorce days, I found myself desperate to keep busy, to stop thinking about my woes.

I must have read every self-help book going, drunk far too much alcohol – despite being not much of a drinker – and I even spent a few days under the duvet, trying to shut out the world by sleeping the time away. There were days when I felt I was coping pretty well; ask anyone who knows me and they'll tell you I was often the life and soul of the party. Yet when I got home, all alone and closed my front door, the eerie silence of my empty flat would hit me from nowhere and I'd be a snivelling wreck once more. I knew this was to be expected, and I knew I had to get through it but I eventually reached a point when loneliness and grief became something deeper and I realised I was getting depressed which is a whole different scenario. I knew I needed professional help.

Calling in the professionals

I knew I'd reached the stage where my state of mind was my enemy and I needed help in sorting myself out. After all, if you break a tooth, you go straight to a dentist so if your mind's in trouble, why not see a therapist? There's still a bit of stigma attached to seeking professional emotional help but honestly, there's no shame in it. I don't mind admitting I saw a counsellor and I'm glad I did. Even though it was Grant's decision to cheat and to ruin our marriage, I felt as if I'd failed somehow. I know now that experiencing feelings of failure after a marriage breakdown is quite normal but at the time, I was overwhelmed by my emotions and needed a trained professional to listen to me and hopefully reassure me that I wasn't going mad and that everything would be ok eventually.

Engaging the right therapist for you is just as important as finding the right solicitor to manage your divorce. You will have a very intense relationship with that person for weeks or months and will need to feel comfortable enough with them to be open and honest about all the issues you're dealing with. I was given some recommendations and also did my own research and I eventually found the right person for me.

I don't mind confessing I am now a fully paid up member of the 'seek help society.' Maybe it's a generation thing and maybe it's a northern thing as well but we're not like America and don't usually rush to get therapy over here. 'No, I'm fine, I don't need any help thank you', but sometimes you do need help as your friends and family can't always provide the answers.

If you seek professional advice it opens up a whole new thought process. The experts make you look at the bigger picture and help open up your mind. It was described to me like this: we're a switchboard and most switchboards can be reprogrammed. Once that happens you can deal with life a lot better. We have this thing called cognitive behaviour so something happens and we react, something else happens and we react. Cognitive behaviour is learnt by years and years of reacting in the same way to various situations but the good news is that it can be unlearnt as long as you make a conscious effort to effect the necessary changes.

The man who voted me off Dancing on Ice is the kindest soul you could ever meet. Thank you Jason Gardiner for being my panto hero.

And so I sought help. I have private medical insurance and I looked at the small print and discovered I could have a thousand pounds of 'shrinkage' on my health plan. I thought I've been paying into this scheme for such a long time I might as well have it and along I went.

I was really frightened about therapy. I felt to start off with that I was giving in, I was weak. That I think is most likely my programming and you could be the same? I was also panicking a little beforehand because I knew I had only an hour's appointment and wondered how I was going to tell this stranger my life story in just sixty minutes.

I got there, took a deep breath and sat down in an armchair. As soon as the therapist, a wonderful man by the name of Doctor Tim Cantopher, asked me why I was there, I started wailing, he passed me the tissues and off we went. He began by asking me questions about myself: was I an organised person? How did I view work? How did I view friends? Then he asked me similar questions about Grant. This went on for about twenty minutes then he spent the next twenty minutes telling me about my life and my marriage as though he actually lived with us. It blew me away, I asked, 'How do you know all this?' and he replied 'Because you may think you're unique but you're not. I've had a thousand Antheas and a thousand Grants sitting in front of me over the years and I can even tell you what's going to happen in the months ahead.' I could have been sitting with Mystic Meg because his predictions were so precise and accurate. He told me, 'Your marriage has lasted this long only because you're a facilitator for bad behaviour. You are a sorter, you're a doer. You run things and you make things better for others. I'm afraid that people like you will always help people like Grant by making everything right; no matter what he does, you will accommodate him. You are a facilitator for his bad behaviour. You have to stop.'

He talked to me about patterned behaviour and said that he could tell me how Grant would behave in the future and to some extent, how I would behave. We examined Grant's business patterns which are all the same and his relationship patterns which are all the same: how he treated Della, how he treated me. And we looked at my patterns of behaviour, how I have always worked and worked at things because of my dyslexia. I always thought I had to work harder than anyone else because of how much I struggled at school. I would do whatever I had to in order to get by. It was almost predestined that I'd end up in a people-pleasing industry using my smile and determination because I was never going to work in an office; never use a pen. That first session was a revelation to me.

I truly believe that therapy opens your mind up to this bigger world of understanding human nature. Once you do, I tell you it's like those are your light bulb moments.

Unfortunately for me, this wise gentleman was retiring after our first session of therapy so I then went to see someone else who was a very nice lady but not very good. I think I ended up hearing more about her life than she did mine and I gave her a few tips. So that didn't last long.

Then I went to a wonderful organisation called Positive Group led by a Doctor Brian Marien. They deal with a lot of people in business, particularly in the City and various companies. I would say to anybody, if there's something you can't deal with, find the right person to help you. I came out of my first session feeling as if I'd had a scientific lecture on the workings of the human mind. I didn't need someone to sit me down with a cup of tea and say, 'Now tell me all about it', because I can get that from my friends. You on the other hand might want or need exactly that so see the right person for you. I needed a greater understanding of where I had been. Where I was and where I was going. Quite a lot of our behaviour stems from our past and I needed that to be explained to me so that I could recognise when I was repeating previous mistakes and so make better life choices.

I had several therapy sessions with Dr Marien and over the months, so many things became clearer to me. He dealt not so much with my problems but helped me understand the workings of the human mind: why we react the way we do; how we can change our reference point and our fears. If you've been doing something the same way for years and years and it's not working for you, then you have change. Thanks to him I did change and realised it wasn't me who was always wrong, and slowly I started to carve the route back to Anthea, Anth, AT and not this woman I didn't recognise. This experience has heightened my empathy and I hate with a passion belittling. In the past when dealing with children I've always been a strong believer in feeding them with realistic confidence, love, humour, conversation and support which delivers a far more rounded adult human. I hadn't been shown kindness or respect by Grant and my past insecurities had surfaced and I had turned into a shadow of my former self.

There was a bit of toing and froing between Grant and myself, we did go out for a meal here and there and we talked. I think this is all part of the process. I won't pretend I wasn't tempted to try and rekindle things and to forgive him yet again, but by then I was strong enough to realise I simply couldn't – for my own well-being. I needed to move on, no matter how much I wanted to believe it would work. Going back would have been wholly the wrong thing to do. It's very difficult because you know this person so well and you want your marriage to succeed. I actually think it's easier if when two people split up, they're immediately with other people and deliriously happy or they simply hate the sight of each other because then there's no looking back. But that wasn't the case for us, so there was this sort of, 'Can we relook at this?' but no, it would have been a huge mistake. I'd learned my lesson, therapy gave me enough power and self-belief to know I could finish the rest of the journey on my own.

There are many pieces of unhelpful advice to which sufferers of depressive illness are prone to be exposed. The commonest and possibly the worst is: "Pull yourself together." If I had a dollar for every time a patient of mine has had this injunction thrown at, I'd be Bill Gates. And it's so pointless. If the sufferer could have pulled himself together he would have done so ages ago. ....what was the object of this stunning gem of advice? Do you really think he is going to put his hand to his brow and gasp: "Gosh thank you so much, I hadn't thought of that. Thank goodness you told me; I'll just go off and sort myself out and then everything will be fine."? I think not.

– from Depressive Illness:
The Curse of the Strong by Dr Tim Cantopher.

I'd tell anyone who's going through a painful and upsetting divorce and looking for some answers on how to go forward, you need to open up your mind and way of thinking, especially if you're in danger of repeating destructive behavioural patterns. This can apply to getting back with an ex who is clearly not right for you or entering new relationships with people who have the same patterns of behaviour that led you to divorcing your ex in the first place. Once you understand why you behaved in a certain way and why that person did, you can learn to change your pattern.

Richard Farleigh an insightful friend I've already mentioned, conducts much of his business life studying patterns. To this hugely successful hedge funder, Chess Grand Master and now private investor I once flippantly said 'You're just good at maths'. 'I am not bad', he replied in his laid back Australian way, 'but that's not what gave me the edge; I'm fascinated by patterns. Countries, companies, individuals, currency, study these in the way I did and you can make some pretty accurate predictions.' Bang, went the 60w bulb in my mind and after that, I couldn't stop thinking about what he said because it made so much sense to me. Everything – and everyone – has a pattern and by switching yourself on to recognise it, you can make calculated predictions about anything, including how a person is likely to behave and how you yourself are likely to behave. So, again, in order to bring about a much-needed change in your behaviour, change your pattern!

Therapy isn't cheap but it shouldn't mean you can't get the help you need. Please, if you're feeling as if you're not coping at all well, then see your GP who can refer you for counselling with an NHS therapist. It may take a bit longer for a referral, but don't give up whatever you do. In the long run you will benefit enormously.

Therapy also has its place for couples going through divorce and can help you achieve a more amicable agreement when it comes to things like joint care of the children and living arrangements. Amelia, Lily and Claudia were old enough that they could talk to me or Grant without us having to tread on eggshells around them. They knew from day one what had happened and reacted to our split in their own way. But younger children need very careful handling. They need to know it's not their fault that their parents aren't staying together anymore and they will need reassurance from both of you that they will be ok, no matter how terrible you're feeling inside. Again, a family therapist can help you. (See Relate, Chapter Two).

Despite the pain of it, this gut-wrenching loneliness is a very normal part of getting over your divorce and it's an illusion. It's part of the story your heart and mind have created to help you deal with what's happening and protect you from further hurt. (The truth is you're never ever completely alone no matter how you feel.)

Everyone deals with their divorce loneliness differently. Some hide in their homes intensifying their loneliness as they watch from their safe place. Others start dating indiscriminately in an effort to feel some sort of connection with just about anyone. Still others disappear into a virtual world of television, social media and online games to fill the void the end of their marriage has left in their lives.

Then there are the lucky ones, like you, who suddenly realise that the only way to stop feeling lonely is to instead feel a sense of belonging and wholeness in yourself. Feeling complete in yourself will prevent you from ever feeling lonely again and can be one of the greatest gifts of divorce.

But there's a bit of a leap from this epiphany and truly leaving your loneliness behind. So, how do you make this leap?

You start with a little logic and let your emotions catch up. Logically, you know there's a BIG difference between being alone and feeling lonely. Being alone is a situation. Feeling lonely is an emotion that's crying out for soothing.

And believe it or not, you can soothe yourself by doing things that indulge your senses. Think about all five of your senses – taste, touch, sight, sound, and smell – and do things that pleasantly engage them.

For example, you might make yourself a fragrant cup of tea to sip, or take a bubble bath surrounded by lit candles while listening to your favourite tunes.

The idea here is to pamper yourself so you feel honoured and valued and whole and loved. And when you're feeling these emotions, it's really difficult to continue to feel loneliness. In fact, when you're feeling these emotions, you feel connected and confident. And confidence is what you need to fully push through the pain of your divorce and heal.

Despite using logic, engaging your senses and letting your emotions shift when you pamper yourself, it's normal to feel loneliness again. It just means that you're not through with your healing and there's more for you to work on.

But each of your successes in acknowledging your loneliness and then consciously choosing to feel differently by soothing yourself will build your belief in the fact that you're just alone and not doomed to be permanently lonely because you've gotten divorced. And as you continue to build this belief you'll soon be able to catch up with the rest of the world and continue on with your life because you've finished mourning the end of your marriage.

Dr Karen Finn

Lara's story...

"Even though I hadn't wanted to divorce Graeme, he left me no choice when he got us into terrible debt through his gambling addiction. I could have coped with losing our house which we did and even with having to take our seven year-old out of the private junior school she was so happy at. What I couldn't deal with were the endless lies and deceit, even after I'd discovered he'd started racking up credit card bills again. He would cry and beg me to forgive him which I did because I still loved him, but after the third time, I went online, downloaded the paperwork and started divorce proceedings.

At first I thought I was managing ok. I'd always worked throughout our ten-year marriage and my parents, who live two roads away, helped me with childcare arrangements for Livy. This didn't change, except now I was renting a two-bedroom flat instead of paying half the mortgage on a four-bedroom detached house and Livy was struggling to fit into her new school where she had no friends. Graeme had to move in with his own parents who weren't particularly happy having him in their spare room and with the help of his boss who luckily was very supportive, he started getting treatment for his addiction. I kept telling myself the only thing that mattered was that we had a roof over our heads and that I had a healthy daughter.

One Saturday evening, out of the blue, I was hit with a tidal wave of despair as I watched television on my own after Livy had gone to sleep. Afterwards I was told I'd most likely had a massive panic attack but at the time I had no idea what was happening to me. I couldn't breathe properly, I felt sick and dizzy and most of all, I felt desperately, desperately sad. Lying on the sofa shaking and crying, it was as though all the emotions of the last few months had come crashing down on me all at once. It's difficult to explain but I was just so lonely; I felt I had no one in the whole world to turn to and if it hadn't have been for Livy, I might even have thought about doing something stupid. My thoughts were irrational but that's what trauma can do to you.

My parents were worried sick. They loaned me some money (which I'm paying back) and I was able to see a counsellor recommended by my GP, on a private basis. It took just over a week to get an appointment and I had six one-hour sessions in all before I felt able to cope on my own again. We talked about everything from my feelings of resentment towards Graeme, our money problems, the effect our divorce was having on our daughter and my own feelings of isolation and failure. I felt I really learned a lot about myself and was able to develop coping mechanisms for the times I found myself slipping into negativity.

Three years on, I'm a different person. I'm stronger and more confident in myself and I feel I'm a better Mum to Livy. I've more or less forgiven Graeme for causing our marriage to break-up and when he recently told me he's got a new girlfriend, I was actually pleased for him. I haven't met anyone else myself yet but if someone were to come into my life, I'm ready."

In a nutshell...

☆ **Divorce is like a death.** It's natural to feel emotions of grief, sadness, despair and anger. They will pass.

☆ **Feelings of loneliness** are normal after divorce and can hit you from nowhere. For the first time in a long time, you are on your own and it can be daunting. Again, you are not alone in feeling this way.

☆ **Talk to friends and family** and keep busy to help you deal with sadness and loneliness.

☆ **Don't suffer in silenc**e if you feel you're not coping. Make an appointment with your GP. There is no shame in doing everything you can to get better.

☆ **Don't underestimate how traumatic divorce can be** for many of us and that some of us need professional help to cope. I don't mind admitting that therapy helped me cope and come to terms with my marriage break-up.

Reunited for a family Christening, post-divorce.

Chapter Five
Friends and Family

From the moment the flag goes up on your divorce, every relationship you have will alter: some better, some worse to a greater or lesser degree. Imagine every app on your phone is wobbling and some you are going to delete, others you need to calm down and a few will get moved to your front page.

They say it's at times of crisis that you learn who your real friends are and I would say from experience that's so true. From learning (from a real friend) that Grant had cheated on me, to returning once more to a position of confidence and strength, I have relied on my friendships to get me through many dark moments. It has taught me whom to trust, whom to steer clear of at certain times and whom I can ring, any time of the day or night. And of course it works both ways – my friends know I'm there for them too.

We women love to talk, to communicate about anything and everything. We enjoy a good gossip and banter and we're there for each other when times are hard. Generally, if a man has a row with his wife, he'll say everything is fine, go off to work and get on with his job as if nothing has happened. Women on the other hand, find it hard to hold it all in and we're in the toilets crying; we want to vent. We all have our go–to girl pals to share bad news with and for me, mine are like a second family I couldn't be without. I call my group of friends my War Cabinet.

Be careful though, of the schadenfreude friends. These are the ones who enjoy another's downfall. They will put their arm around you, ask sympathetically how you're feeling and all the while be lapping up your heartbreak with glee. You become a soap opera for others' enjoyment. When you're hurting, it's very tempting to be too honest and to literally spill your guts to anyone who wants to pull up a pew and listen. But you have to be tempered in certain company and not risk becoming a focus of gossip for everyone's delectation. Choose wisely who to tell your most intimate break-up details to because not only do you not want to be the latest water cooler topic, you risk personal details getting out and into the wrong ears. My wiring because of being in the media business for decades is to be careful of what I divulge outside my close friendship group. I've learned the hard way that being too open can lead to stories mysteriously appearing in newspapers before I've been ready to make them public knowledge myself. So when it came to splitting with Grant, I was ultra-cautious about what I did and didn't say and to whom. In a way that added to my stress because I was maintaining a façade, especially with work colleagues.

The ex

Who knows, your feelings of bitterness towards your ex may change over time and all the venomous details you've divulged about him to your pals, you may wish you had not shared with certain 'friends.' True friends will conveniently forget what you've said and never mention it again if circumstances have changed and you want to start afresh. But others may hold it against you and choose to remind you of every last detail, even when you're desperate to put the past behind you. So again, choose carefully those you can trust and cry with, safe in the knowledge nothing you say will go any further. Be aware of friends who come bearing wine and twenty Marlborough and expect you to dish the dirt. This makes them feel better but in the long run, you won't be helped.

As tempting as it might be, don't be too derogatory about your ex in front of the kids, even if he has cheated on you and is now shacked up with a bimbo young enough to be his daughter. No matter what one parent has done, generally speaking children love both of you and don't want to have to choose. It's hard to know exactly what they're feeling deep down but they won't want to hear you and your friends criticising their Dad so if you do feel the need to rant about your ex, make sure they're out of earshot. It's very easy for a group of girlfriends to get together, break open the wine and spend the evening tearing the cheating other-half to shreds. And it certainly feels good if it's your other-half that's at the receiving end. But children, especially younger ones, think differently and won't want to be forced to take sides. In fact some of the divorced women I spoke to when researching this book, say their children resented them for breaking up the marriage, even though it was their husbands who'd cheated or chosen to leave! Not logical I know but when emotions are involved, logic often goes out of the window and there were times I sailed close to the wind.

In our case, the girls were not children when Grant and I separated – not that they were any less hurt or devastated that the family was breaking up. But it did mean they understood what was happening and they – quite rightly – were bloody angry. They love their Dad of course and there's never been a question of them cutting him out of their lives, but it doesn't mean he got off scot free. What they said to him and how he explained his behaviour to his daughters is between them. But having them in my life made me realise it wouldn't do me any good in the long run to cut their father out of the picture, because I'm the one who could end up suffering. Think of all the occasions which lie ahead of you all – school parents' evenings, recitals, sports fixtures, graduations, weddings, Christenings... the list is endless and you don't want to risk missing out on any of it. I knew that if I followed my gut instinct and never spoke to Grant again, there was a chance I would be excluded from many happy family occasions in the future. This is not because the girls wouldn't want me there – I know I'm very important to all three of them and a huge part of their lives

– but because sometimes they'd have to choose between Grant and I and inevitably, there would be times they'd choose him. Similarly, I know they'd want to invite me to certain things and Grant would be the one left off the guest list so he'd suffer too. So putting aside all my dark thoughts and anger, I made a conscious decision to let go. I'm not pretending it was easy – it wasn't – but forgiveness is a great strength and I'm a stronger woman for it. We communicate now – with the occasional spat for sport – on a normal basis for these reasons. We share a history, we share many friends. Grant's family is my family and has been loving and supportive to me throughout all the dramas. We love the girls and fully intend to be with them on their life's journey.

A friend of mine who'd been divorced herself for many years gave me a good piece of advice which I'm passing on: don't alienate yourself, no matter how hurt you're feeling right now. So many divorces are acrimonious and it's easy to see why; feelings have been trampled on, lives have been torn apart and futures taken away. No wonder one or both parties are left feeling bitter and vengeful. But as I've already stated, forgiveness is a great strength while hatred (such a strong word) can be debilitating and draining. By holding on to that negativity, you can find yourself all alone in your angry little bubble while everyone else around you gets on with their lives. At the end of the day, it's you who will end up the loser and haven't you lost enough already?

Or putting it bluntly, it's better to be on the inside pissing out than the outside pissing in!!

Speaking of losses, many women I've spoken to have told me about friendships lost after divorce – another fallout from a broken marriage. Why is it that when you're no longer a couple, invitations from certain people rapidly dry up? My theory is that some women see a suddenly single woman as a threat to her own marriage; as if this heart–broken, under–confident divorcee is going to pounce on the nearest man, whether he's taken or not. I'm sure there are women out there who are desperate to fill the void their ex has left, as quickly as possible. But the likelihood is, if you're just coming out of a marriage with all the hurt and confusion that entails, you're simply not ready to jump back into another relationship. All you want from your married friends is their friendship, nothing more.

After years of socialising as a couple, it can be incredibly difficult to find yourself the only one in your 'couples circle' without a partner at dinner parties and functions. If there isn't a single man available to 'make up the numbers' you're going to mess up the seating plan, hence another reason that invitation to that dinner party you heard about on the grapevine, didn't land on your doormat.

Some people find it difficult to know how to deal with the separate halves of a divorced couple – where do their loyalties lie? It's a bit like who gets custody of the dog – who gets custody of the friends? I've personally not lost a 'real' friend over my divorce because I was the one in our marriage who made and nurtured the friendships. But there were a few casualties along the way I have to admit. I'm not overly concerned about those people because they weren't genuine friends. When they stopped calling and inviting me to things I realised that you can't control everything and other people. If they want to make an effort with you then that's great; I wasn't going to be the one to end the friendship. But if they couldn't deal with me and Grant splitting up for whatever reason, then fine. As I've already said, you soon find out who your true friends are and I know who mine are and feel thankful for them every day.

Aimee's story...

"I lost a number of so—called friends when Gareth and I split up. We belonged to what I believed was a close—knit group of couples, who we socialised with regularly, yet they stopped inviting me along to things when Gareth left me. It's true I'm the one who instigated the divorce — only because he'd admitted to having affairs — but I felt like I was the one being punished for some reason.

Months later one of the women in the group who didn't desert me, admitted that Gareth had been telling everyone I'd caused our marriage problems and had met someone else — all lies. Our friends believed him and took his side, yet they hadn't bothered to speak to me to get my version.

To be honest, I don't care anymore. It was hurtful at the time but they obviously weren't real friends or else they'd have stood by me no matter what. It's so true you do learn who's genuine when you're going through tough times. "

Me and Sally through thick
and thin.

Get practical

Not long after Grant and I had split, Sally Meen, shocked by my weight loss, literally bundled me in her car and drove me to the supermarket. She bought me loads of food, filled up my fridge, cooked me dinner and urged me to eat. Like a lot of people, I don't eat when I'm miserable. When the singer Cheryl Fernandez Versini filed for divorce, she claimed in her petition that she'd lost weight due to the stress of her ex's unreasonable behaviour. And if you look back at pictures of her at this time, you'll see she actually did look terrible, all skin and bones. That's me. The last thing I want when I'm really in trouble is food and as I'm not huge anyway, it doesn't take long before I begin to look and feel ill. I can't help it; I've always been this way but it's not healthy. I don't recommend the stress diet to anyone.

Don't be afraid to ask for help. If for example you need the name of a good solicitor, counsellor, therapist or whatever, one of your friends may well know someone. We all get different things from different people. For instance, one of my friends is a great divorce lawyer and she was one of the first people I called when I knew Grant and I were over for good. You can read her contribution to this book in Chapter Three.

Random acts of kindness are treasures of the soul. So many people did little things that meant so much. My colourist Imogen turned up with a bunch of flowers and insisted I accepted her turning me into a natural blond as a gift. Jill

Me, Sally and my Goddaughter Tilly

Zander who owned my local beauty salon in Esher hauled me in and insisted on putting my face back together with every machine and potion she had at her disposal, a black cab driver in London said you've had a rough time babe have this one on me, friends sent me messages and ones I hadn't heard from in ages just knew I needed support. Lots of people simply did lovely, unexpected things which helped me more than I can say.

"There is nothing better than a friend,
unless it is a friend with chocolate."
– Linda Grayson

Other friends will do sleight of hand. They'll engage you in a project or an issue of their own and distract you from your misery. Then there are those friends who are just there and will listen quietly, letting you cry and talk into the night, often without needing to say anything. I remember sitting in a room when it all kicked off between me and Grant the first time. It was morning and I sat there until it started to get dark outside. I felt an absolute failure as the horrible truth sank in, as if I'd done something wrong. As I've already mentioned, I spoke to just one person that whole day, Madoc Bellamy, who has since sadly passed away. He just listened to me on the 'phone as I said everything I probably wanted to say to Grant but couldn't. I must have spoken to him about three separate times that day until I finally fell asleep with emotional exhaustion. He didn't judge me, he didn't judge Grant and he didn't offer me any solutions. He simply listened and that was exactly what I needed at that time. Sometimes all you want is a list of numbers so you can call a pal if you're having a bad day. Don't be ashamed or embarrassed to pick up the phone and make that call if you need to.

A particularly dear friend whom I did call upon is Steve Chalke, a Baptist minister who went on to found Christian charity Oasis Trust in 1985. We met when he joined GMTV during my time as anchor and I have always cherished his friendship. When my head becomes muddled, Steve has always been there with his wise words and clear explanations and he offered me solace when I really needed it after Grant and I split up.

One conversation with him went something like this: 'Imagine in life we each have a book, it's our real story, our soul story and because we are all on a journey, outside influences write across our pages some good, some bad, but we should always be tweaking and editing our book as a good objective editor would. Negativity though is powerful and sometimes throws us off our game, makes us lose our thread, brings in doubt, and then our book becomes confusing.

'Look at the child who comes into this world full of hope and optimism but instead of being born to good loving parents who encourage and nurture that child, they are belittled, told they are naughty, unintelligent, a problem. So that child withdraws, starts to crumble inside until so much damage is done they believe these words which have been written in their book and they become what they have been told. But it's not the truth and they don't know how to edit the words out.

'We can all relate to that analogy but that same chain of events can happen to adults and we get what we are expecting which is sadness and failure; we reap what we sow. I'm not saying this is easy, it's one of the hardest things you'll ever do, but you have to change your story and ruthlessly edit out everything that's been scribbled over your soul that's negative and drains you and go through that soul book until you have returned it to your story and not someone else's.'

"Friends are the family we choose for ourselves."
— Edna Buchanan

Family

Thankfully, I have a solid relationship with my ex's family. They are still family to me and they always will be. Of course things change when you break up with your partner and somewhere along the line you have to make a new life of your own but it's easier all round if you can stay civil. After all, it's not the fault of anyone else that your marriage didn't work out so what would be the point of alienating your in–laws? If you have children, the chances are they will have a vested interest in them and quite often you'll find they are feeling as vulnerable as you are because they'll be worried about seeing less of you if you are the 'injured' party and of their nieces, nephews or grandchildren.

Marrying someone means you are inextricably intertwined with so many others and that includes parents–in–laws, the siblings of your other half, and even their grandparents. The fall–out from a divorce can be far–reaching and difficult to come to terms with which is even more reason to hold on to good family relationships. If you have young children, don't 'punish' anyone by trying to stop them from seeing a grandparent or aunt or uncle, no matter how much you might despise their Dad right now. It can be heart breaking for relatives to suddenly lose contact with their loved ones and children especially will suffer if their extended family is reduced overnight.

*"I sustain myself with
the love of family."*
– Maya Angelou

One woman I spoke to admitted to me she was so bitter after her husband walked out on her and their young daughter that she did everything in her power to hurt him and used their three year–old to do it. She started by refusing to allow her heartbroken mother–in–law to spend any time with her granddaughter, stopping her from collecting her from nursery twice a week. She knew she'd rile her ex by her actions – it worked – but it also hurt her mother in–law and her small daughter who adored each other. It was only when her mother and father in–law both appeared on her doorstep one evening, literally in tears begging to talk things through that she realised how wrong she'd been and how she'd needlessly hurt people she cared about and who cared about her.

Me, Claudia and Amelia.

This is me, Claudia and Lily so there
are no arguments!

Molly's story

"When I married my best friend's brother Chris twenty years ago, we all used to joke that if we ever split up, there would be hell to pay. Sandie is incredibly close to Chris — they're a very close-knit family — and over the years I realised there were certain things I couldn't tell either one of them if I wanted it to remain secret.

So when Chris and I began to have marital problems, I kept a lot of the details to myself. I knew Sandie would always support me, we'd been friends since the first day of senior school, but blood is thicker than water and I couldn't be entirely sure she would necessarily take my side if push came to shove.

Six months later, I found out Chris had been having an affair with a mutual friend and I was devastated. I called Sandie in floods of tears, barely able to get the words out. I thought she'd be furious with her brother but her reaction stunned me: she'd already known about the affair and admitted she thought it would all just fizzle out. What's more, she said she thought Chris was under stress and acting out of character and that I needed to give him some space. What!

I'd always felt amazingly lucky to be part of such a close, loving family. We'd all enjoyed countless family functions and holidays together but at that point I realised I was an outsider. I bet if I'd been the one to have the affair, everyone would have rallied round Chris and I'd have been made to feel a pariah. Yet here they were making excuses for Chris's bad behaviour! I just couldn't believe Sandie could take her brother's side on this. She insisted that she wasn't and that she was 'disappointed' in him, but I certainly didn't feel she had my back and that was almost as heart breaking as discovering my husband was a cheat.

Chris and I never had children — not for want of trying — so in a way, it felt easier to end our marriage. Perhaps if we'd had kids to consider we — or I — would have tried harder to work through our problems. He claimed he didn't want to be with this other woman and loved me, but I was just so hurt and humiliated, I didn't want to even consider taking him back.

Sandie naturally, blamed me, especially when Chris begged her to 'talk me round' and I stood by my decision to file for divorce. So I ended up losing a husband, best friend and 'family' all in one go. Perhaps if Sandie and my in-laws had behaved more like a real family to me and given me the support I needed at the time, it could have worked out differently."

Jodie's story...

"When I discovered my husband Marcus was not only cheating on me but using our hard-earned money to buy extravagant gifts for his mistress, I went absolutely crazy. In a blind fury, I stuffed his clothes into black bin liners and hurled them outside on the driveway then called every member of his family to make sure they all knew what a bastard he'd been. I accused them of covering for Marcus and betraying me, none of which I had any evidence to support. I had every right to be furious — he behaved badly and hurt me terribly — but in hindsight, I overreacted. Marcus's Mum and Dad had always treated me like a daughter and I know if I'd sat down and spoken to them rationally, they would have been supportive towards me. Instead I ranted and raved about their son's misdemeanours, until eventually our relationship became strained and difficult. It wasn't their fault Marcus had strayed, yet I took out my anger on them which was wrong of me. No one was to blame except Marcus.

Thankfully, relations between us are much more cordial now, two years on. I've apologised many times for the way I acted and they do understand why I behaved the way I did. They dote on our teenage children and they're always happy to babysit if I want to go out. Marcus and I don't speak — I still can't forgive him for breaking up our marriage — but I'm so grateful his family are there for me and the kids."

Anjie's story...

"I'm not proud of myself but it was basically my fault my marriage broke down and I ended up a divorcee and single Mum of two. I had a mad, crazy affair with a work colleague and got caught. I broke my husband Stefan's heart and hurt my children when Stefan rightly left me, yet amazingly, my in-laws stood by me and never judged. Not ever.

Looking back, I still can't believe I was such a fool. I wasn't unhappily married, yet I went looking for that extra bit of excitement. I thought I could have a 'secret' fling without anyone getting hurt but of course it doesn't work that way. Stefan's no fool: it must have been so obvious what I was up to when I started going out 'with the girls' more and more. Sure enough, one evening he was waiting up for me and it was evident he knew what I'd been up to. He was absolutely devastated when I admitted everything and as far as he was concerned, there was no room for second chances. Of course I knew immediately I'd made a terrible mistake but it was all too late. Stefan filed for divorce and we had to sell the house.

It all happened so quickly, I didn't have time to think. If it hadn't have been for his lovely, warm, Italian parents who were more forgiving than my own Mum and Dad, I don't know what I'd have done. They never stopped calling me or visiting and they made it easy for me to see them because they refused to take sides or blame me. They dote on the children and they carried on babysitting whenever I asked and spoiling them with treats.

They're wonderful people and I'm so blessed to have them in my life. I feel as if I don't deserve their respect and affection but they still call me their daughter and as far as I'm concerned, they'll always be my family."

Me and Claudia

Chapter Six
Still I Rise

Journalist Angella Johnson sent me a copy of the poem *Still I Rise* by Maya Angelou when she heard about my divorce from Grant. She knew I didn't want to talk — that wasn't the point. It was meant for me to read and take comfort and inspiration from which I did, often. It was lovely of her and the poem has meant a great deal to me ever since. In fact the title became my mantra for a while as I was trying to get my life back on track and is now the perfect heading for this part of the 'surviving divorce' journey.

As already touched upon in Chapter Three, you may feel that the end of your marriage means the end of your dreams. Everything's gone up and cascaded down and nothing's the same any more. But you have to rise from the ashes like a phoenix. As I have discovered myself, divorce can lead to all sorts of new beginnings - a new career, renewed friendships, brand new friendships, a new partner perhaps, and a fresh approach to life.

Whether or not you wanted a divorce, it has happened and it is time to accept there are things you cannot change, no matter how much you may want to. You're experiencing a gauntlet of emotions — grief, loss, sadness, fear, loneliness, failure and heartache — and yes, no one is pretending you're going to suddenly wake up and be back to 'normal'. It takes time and it takes effort on your part to put the past behind you and start living again. Now is the time to take your future into your own hands and do everything in your power to get your life back. Make that effort. You're in a sink or swim situation and you know it's the right thing to do.

I think it's important to understand that you're actually ok. We all have destructive thoughts from time to time and we're all very good at thumbing through the back chapters of our life book when we should be writing the next one. Now is the time to change all that and make progress. This chapter is about you learning to be on your own and getting back to the person you really are instead of the machine you've had to become. It's about regaining your self-esteem, feeling attractive and confident again. If you want to take 'revenge' (we're human after all) this is the way to do it - be happy.   It's like any new challenge in life: you have to force yourself to adopt the right mind set and use sheer determination to achieve your goals.

"Some people work at
being miserable.
I work at being happy."
– Dolly Parton

I think the most difficult thing is letting go. Extricating oneself from the past, from the 'way things used to be' and deciding once and for all that from now on, life is going to be different, yes, but better. Your past should make you better, not bitter is now your mantra.

If you're struggling to manage without 'him' because you miss the things you used to do together and doing them alone makes you feel sad - change your routine. Consign memories of your coupledom to the past and create new memories for yourself. No one's saying it will be easy but if you are going to move on and rise again, only you can take the steps to make that happen. It might mean getting a new job, moving to a different area, cutting certain reminders (including unhelpful people) out of your life or taking up a new pursuit, something that's not associated with your ex. It could also be as simple as redecorating your bedroom, rearranging the furniture or starting to retrain for something.

In my case, one of the first things I did was to have a 'declutter'. It's not surprising really is it, considering I once presented a whole TV series based on the concept? I've always believed in keeping a tidy home but this was different. It wasn't just the house I was cleansing but my headspace as well. I didn't even realise I needed it until my youngest step daughter Claudia took me in hand and said, 'Right, we're having a clear-out and starting with your wardrobe!' We're not all wired in the same way and you might not have the energy or inclination to start spring cleaning when you're worrying about paying the bills but I can't stress enough the cleansing effect that a good old clear out can have on a person. If it doesn't come naturally to you, find a friend to help you because trust me, your brain might be jumbled up with all sorts of thoughts churning around, but having an ordered and organised living space goes a long way to helping you to clear your thoughts. If it's not beautiful, useful or seriously sentimental get rid of it. I gave these words to a contestant on *Perfect Housewife* and she got rid of her husband because as she explained, she couldn't actually put him in either category.

On Perfect Housewife burning an
emblem of pain !!

> "When we clear the physical
> clutter from our lives,
> we literally make
> way for inspiration and 'good,
> orderly direction' to enter."
> **– Julia Cameron**

Claudia is the 'baby' of the family and until the point she took me in hand, it was always me dishing out the good advice: how the tables had turned. A few days before we moved into our new apartment, she started rummaging through my wardrobe. I thought I'd already got rid of everything of no use out but apparently not. She went through each item I possessed saying things like, 'Nope, too Mumsy'; 'nope, hate that'; 'hmmm, that's not too bad...' I must have lost about forty per cent of my clothes to the local charity shop and funnily enough, to Claudia's own wardrobe, but it wasn't a bad thing. It was quite comforting in a way because all of a sudden I was being advised. Someone was helping me and telling me what to do and I was grateful. Very freely and brutally she gave me the benefit of her opinions. She was very wise and she knew I needed help. Not only did I have a nice neat wardrobe, but also a lot to think about.

That little session though did strangely change our dynamic. Claudia has been in my life since she was two and I'd always been the one to help her but now I often ask for and truly value her advice.

A good old turf out can be very empowering. Whether you're staying in the marital home or moving to a new place, rip through not just your wardrobe – although it's a great place to start – but each and every drawer and shelf in your home. If you're still harbouring items that cause you pain when you look at them, such as the wedding album, your wedding dress or maybe a particular wedding gift, now is the time to clear it out. I'm not suggesting you throw everything away: they may conjure up happy memories one day in the future; just put them away for now. My beautiful wedding gown which I wore on that glorious day in August 2000 is actually packed away in Grant's garage along with lots of photo albums, because I don't have room for them in my flat. I don't care about them right now but one day I might retrieve everything to relieve the good bits of our marriage. Or I might not.

When I was presenting *Perfect Housewife* some years back, I met a woman who lived in a three-bedroomed house in Doncaster. She was a divorcee and lived with her two sons. She used her third bedroom as a storage area. It was full of stuff she didn't want or use and she rarely went in there. When I asked her why she didn't simply clear it out and allow the boys to each have their own bedroom, she admitted it was full of wedding memorabilia and she couldn't bear to look at it. What a waste of space! Her marriage had been unhappy for a long time before her divorce and she was now in a new relationship which was going well. I asked her if she had a BBQ which she did and between us, we piled up all the things which were making her miserable – including her wedding dress – and together we watched them all go up in flames. There were literally tears of sheer relief and delight on her face. Her house had needed cleansing and purging and she'd just needed a gentle push to help her do it so she could embrace her new life. That bit wasn't transmitted because it wasn't what the show was about but we did reveal how lovely her home looked afterwards with all three bedrooms being used properly and more importantly, how happy she was that she'd finally had the courage to let go of her past.

"Sometimes you have to let everything go – purge yourself. If you are unhappy with anything – whatever is bringing you down – get rid of it. Because you will find that when you are free, your true creativity, your true self comes out."
– Tina Turner

♥ ♥ ♥

Get the look

You might not be feeling very attractive right now but don't abandon yourself. No matter how hard it is, force yourself to eat well and to take care of your appearance. It's amazing how putting on a clean pair of jeans and a lick of lipstick can make you look – and feel – a million dollars. A lot of women opt for a drastic hair cut after a big life change such as starting or losing a job or losing weight. Or getting a divorce and it's easy to understand why. A great hairstyle can transform your whole look and help you regain a little bit of confidence. So if you can afford to do it, make that appointment. Get the roots done, go blonde if you've been toying with the idea for ages but haven't had the guts – why not? It's a small gesture in the scheme of things but we're women and that's the way we roll.

While you're at it, why not update your wardrobe? Again, it doesn't have to be expensive. Not many have bottomless bank accounts, especially when the finances have just been split in two. But there are bargains to be had everywhere. The high street has never been so good and there seem to be sales on frequently. If necessary, enlist the help of a friend who has a good eye for style, we all have one, and she'll be happy to see you as her new project and for you it will be a distraction from the upheaval you're going through. The next time you see your ex you want to look your best. There's no harm whatsoever in letting him see the gorgeous woman he's lost.

If you've been meaning to lose weight, now is the time to do it. A friend of mine found herself at a loose end whenever her ex had the children and so took up running to take her mind off the fact that she was a single mother and a fed-up one. She simply bought herself a pair of trainers and a plastic water bottle and began pounding the pavements and fields whenever she felt a wave of loneliness hit her. Gradually she found herself actually looking forward to those sessions out in the fresh air with nothing to think about but the next step. She lost lots of weight and looked and felt fantastic. She also cleared her mind of all the negative thoughts which had been haunting her and emerged after six or seven months, a fitter, leaner, stronger version of herself. Personally, I've always exercised because it makes me feel good no matter what's happening in my life. Exercise releases endorphins which are the body's natural feel-good chemicals. I often went out running in all weathers when Grant and I split up. I found it therapeutic and keeping fit has to be a good thing.

Years ago, before my own divorce, I met a friend at a wedding who I hadn't seen for ages and she looked amazing. She put her fabulous figure down to 'The Divorce Diet', saying she'd lost a pound for every year of her marriage – fourteen – and felt wonderful. Her husband, by the way, had suffered a midlife crisis and left her for a twenty-seven year-old, disappearing off to the US with not a lot of thought for their two young children or the mortgage. After years of struggling on all fronts, Jo is now one of the most capable, empathetic, sexy, confident women I know and her transformation was helped enormously by looking good and therefore feeling good. Her weight loss went a long way to boosting her confidence enough to turn her life around and by God she has.

Blue jobs and pink jobs

One of the most difficult aspects of living alone was having to do things I'd never had to do for myself. I'd gone from Dad to boyfriend to husband. When you're in a relationship, over time you tend to carve out the jobs between the two of you, not because you're incapable in any way but because often it makes sense that one of you does certain things like change a car tyre (him) buys the Christmas presents (me). I call them blue jobs and pink jobs and I know I'm not alone because many of the women I've spoken to about this agree that tasks like taking out the bins or making a doctor's appointment for one of the children is often gender-related.

I'll give you a silly example. When I was with Grant and I'd broken down with a flat tyre while out on my own, I would have called him and asked him to come out to help me. He would have raced out and taken over my car, allowing me to drive his home while he sorted out the flat tyre. Had this happened a few months after our break-up, emotionally wrecked, I would probably have burst into pathetic tears while struggling with how to deal with the problem and who I was going to ring. Now though, everything's different and I deal with my changing circumstances much better. Only a few months ago around 11pm while driving home I had a blowout and my tyre was losing pressure at a rapid rate – damn those kerb stones that jump out and grab hold of your wheel. I calmly pulled over, Googled the nearest twenty-four-hour tyre service, gave them my precise location and within an hour, I was back on the road heading home. There was no drama. It might sound like a small victory but I was proud of myself for simply handling the situation without feeling the need to ring a friend as I might once have done. I know I can look after myself and get through tricky situations. There's something strangely empowering when you realise there's very little you can't handle, from a broken boiler to cutting the grass. I'm even the proud owner of my own drill and set of raw plugs – a far cry from the old me! It's vital to step out of your comfort zone and learn to look after yourself. What's more, even if there was someone else on the scene, it's a good feeling knowing you don't actually need anyone else to get you through life's challenges. Even if you delegate tasks which I often do, you're still in charge and none of this means losing an ounce of your femininity.

I was introduced to a fantastic life coach about a year ago, by the name of Sarah Jones. I feel she deserves to be included in this book because not only did she help me enormously in coming to terms with my changed circumstances, empowering me and supporting me, but she spends her life helping endless other women going through the aftermath of divorce. She's a divorcee herself and a single Mum and knows only too well what a s*** time it is, even if you're the one who wanted out of your marriage.

Sarah's story

"I'm someone who has been there, done that and now makes the t-shirts. I always tell myself I'm 'not broken, just remodelled'; I've lost a marriage, not myself. My mother always taught me, 'Even in the hardest times, we should reach into ourselves, find strength and continue living the best life possible'.

When I finally figured out that no one else was responsible for my happiness, I felt invigorated at the thought of making myself happy after all these years of fighting for an ill-fated marriage. I was exhausted from the horrible ending to my marriage. I was really starting to feel hopeful that I had this awesome chance at creating a new me again! Maybe I could finally be happy, I thought. But what does that mean? It means different things to different people. Only you have to wake up and go to bed being you every day.

When we're children, fairy tales teach us that sad stories have happy endings. Children's books are peopled by good people who are rewarded and by evil people who are punished. In an ideal world this would be true, too, and there would always be happy endings. Marriages would last forever and husbands and wives would live in peace, contentment, and fidelity. This is not an ideal world, however, and this is true whether we are the one who got left or whether we are the one who does the leaving.

You don't go through a divorce and come out without scars. So much of your time, of your energy, and of yourself went into the building of the partnership that when the partnership is destroyed, you are forever changed. And before you can be truly free to move on, you must learn to accept the transformation in your identity and in your way of life that has been brought about by the breakdown of your relationship.

When my divorce came through, I was a person again. Now, I look on the marriage as a period in my life that came to an end. Complete inner acceptance and the knowledge that life has another purpose.

For the first year I didn't know who I was now because of these new labels – single mother, ex-wife. O.K, pain follows divorce! You have to feel it, process it, and expect it to not go away just because you want it to. There is the death of a dream in this for many of us – and that too is hard. I've realised that sadness is going to accompany a divorce for a while until it doesn't. I have painted, kept a journal; run; lifted weights;

prayed; meditated; lit things on fire and talked until I can't stand hearing my own voice. Time does heal. Keeping busy does help. Focusing on what you have to do helps. Learning to live with the sadness feels a lot better than fighting it.

I don't want my ex-husband back. I don't ever want to live with him again. I am so glad that part of my life is over. It was miserable. I was miserable. The cheating and leaving were just sticky icing on the bitter cake. I think one of the hardest things to come to grips with is the loss of the future, the loss of the family you had pictured in your head. When things are not what they appear you start to question everything about that old life, was it all a lie? I have asked myself that a million times.

Consider this period a time-out, a time for sowing the seeds for new growth. You can emerge from this experience knowing yourself better and feeling stronger. We must take the primary responsibility for our own self-worth and our own expectations; being able to live by this understanding is to know real freedom.

The most important thing I've learned is the key to everything else: to learn to love yourself. I believe it's what has made a difference in my life. I never thought that being a divorcee would be such a big part of my self-identity. I don't feel bad or ashamed or anything like that; it's just that if I had to describe myself, I'd say that   I am someone who endures. I'm no longer a wife, but the afterimage of that identity remains. After divorce, you have the opportunity and freedom to become who you wish to be. You should use this opportunity, no matter how negative its origins, to resurrect your identity and exercise freedom of choice. Seize the chance to create and learn, and use your experiences as a means of building something new.

Think about who you want to be, the person you were before the marriage, or maybe a new person? What are some of the things you can do differently? Look for changes you can say yes to, instead of dwelling on what's out of reach. When I cleared away the negative emotions and came to terms with the stigma imposed by the outside world, I had the freedom to begin again without constraint and to do with my life what I wanted to do with it.

No matter how glorious, and perhaps unrealistic, these words may sound, it can be done. It has been done by many others who have been through divorce they thought they might never survive and have gone on to achieve great things.

Regardless of whether you choose your divorce or not, divorce means it's time for a change. It's time to remodel. It's time to take a look at what needs to be stripped down and refinished, what needs to be renovated, what can stay, and perhaps what should be torn down and totally rebuilt. Whatever kind of changes your divorce requires, the key concept here is that YOU get to choose how your life gets rebuilt.

I used divorce as an opportunity for growth and maturity. To move my life forward, it had to start by focusing on me. But however you get there, the question now is where do you go from here? And how do you figure out who you are and what you want as a newly single person? What is your new life going to look like, and how do you start moving in that direction?

To move your life forward, it is important to acknowledge your feelings and to learn from your feelings and to learn from your past experiences to prepare yourself for the next exciting chapter of your life, Yes, there is life after divorce. Learn to let the past go! Just, let it go."

I'm very fortunate because in my line of work I get introduced to so many interesting people and Sarah is one of the best. She has helped literally hundreds of both men and women and had already worked her magic on a few people I know, not just through life coaching but also Intuitive Healing which she specialises in. A mutual friend could see I was very tense one day and struggling with any number of things going on in my life and put me together with Sarah. I haven't looked back since and in fact she has become a good friend. She takes a very personal, holistic approach and gradually helped me see things differently, more positively. I have her to thank for 'rising again' and taking back control of my life. As you'll gather from her own story, she's been through the mill herself and is very wise.

Sarah's details are listed at the back of the book but for now, here are some of her words of wisdom...

In a nutshell...

☆ **It's time to put you first.** Basically, it's up to you. You've got to find something that makes you feel good about you and do it.

☆ **Acceptance of your identity** post-divorce is the final stage of your recovery. Full recovery is accepting that your experience is part of what you are rather than being something that happened to you in the past.

☆ **After divorce**, you have the opportunity and freedom to become who you wish to be. Seize the chance to create and learn, and use your experiences as a means of building something new.

☆ **Rediscover who you used to be.** Especially if you were married for a long time, you may have given up a lot of the things you enjoyed as a single person because they didn't fit with being 'a couple'. Do them now.

☆ **Discover a new side of yourself.** The life-changing period of divorce, though often difficult and unwelcome, holds a silver lining: shake things up and try on a new lifestyle.

☆ **Dare to be alone.** Being alone doesn't mean being isolated and never seeing anyone. It just means not being coupled up, or in a rush to do so.

☆ **Forgiveness.** My response to people encouraging me to forgive was one of indignation. How could I be expected to forgive? But they were right. By refusing to forgive, I wasn't hurting him, I was hurting me. Forgiving him was a gift of peace to myself.

☆ **Grasping.** When we lose everything, it is human nature to grasp onto whatever remains, including pain. It's tempting to stay in pain, but is that really what you want?

☆ **Associations.** Do you have triggers that are like a time warp to the past, pulling you back to moments of agony and anxiety? I do. Triggers and associations are not inevitable; you can retrain your brain. It takes work. But it's worth it.

☆ **Self-care.** You may now bear the sole burden of your children's well-being and so you push your own care to the side. But in order to be the best parent you can be, you have to be the best person you can be. And that means taking care of yourself and your needs.

☆ **I cannot change my ex.** It's normal to want to have a say in how your ex behaves, particularly related to the children. But save yourself the struggle. Unless he is abusing the kids or repeatedly not showing up, you can't generally control his actions

☆ **Ten minutes a day can make a difference.** You deserve to do something special for yourself every day, even if only for ten minutes. It can be as simple as taking a walk or reading a book.

☆ **Lighten-up!** Life after divorce usually means added responsibilities. How do you handle it all without being totally stressed out? To start, learn to laugh more, especially at yourself. Learn to let things go and not take life so seriously.

☆ **What makes you truly happy?** What do you feel is your true purpose in life? Knowing your purpose, will give you a true sense of who you are and how you are supposed to make a difference in the world. It's your compass!

☆ **Recognise that it's OK to have different feelings.** It's normal to feel sad, angry, exhausted, frustrated, and confused. You also may feel anxious about the future. Accept that reactions like these will lessen over time.

☆ **Give yourself a break.** Give yourself permission to feel and to function at a less than optimal level for a period of time. No one is superman or superwoman; take time to heal, regroup, and re-energise.

☆ **Don't go through this alone.** Sharing your feelings with friends and family can help you get through this period. Consider joining a support group where you can talk to others in similar situations.

☆ **Remember that moving on is the end goal.** Expressing your feelings is liberating but getting stuck in negative emotions like blame, anger, and resentment will rob you of valuable energy and prevent you from healing and moving forward.

☆ **Remind yourself that you still have a future.** As you grieve the loss of the future you once envisioned, be encouraged by the fact that new hopes and dreams will eventually replace your old ones.

☆ **Spend time with loved ones**, people who support, value, and energise you. Surround yourself with people who are positive and who truly listen to you.

☆ **Cultivate new friendships.** If you feel like you have lost your social network along with the divorce or breakup, make an effort to meet new people. Join a networking group or special interest club, take a class, get involved in community activities...

☆ **Take a time out.** Try not to make any major decisions in the first few months after a separation or divorce, like starting a new job or moving to a new city. If you can, wait until you're feeling less emotional so that you can make better decisions.

☆ **The List:** Start by making a list of the top five things that would make you happy right now. Rome wasn't built in a day, just pick five. Keep it simple; let's take this one day at a time. Make it tangible, feasible and fun!

☆ **Complete the list:** It is one thing to write down the list and another to follow through on its content. This should be easy as your list is small right now. First take a deep breath, remember this is a new journey.

☆ **Journal:** Start keeping a journal as you embark on the road to happiness. It is really amazing to read back and reflect on how much your mood has changed.

Peter, me and Grant

Chapter Seven
Dating Again

When it comes to the whole business of dating, I have to admit this is not my area of expertise. In fact I am pretty rubbish when it comes to the opposite sex and all I can offer you in this chapter is the benefit of my own, somewhat limited, experiences of dating and those of friends I've spoken to on the subject. Many women I know have a completely different approach to dating than I have and who's to say if their take is any more or less successful than mine?

To be absolutely honest here, I've never, ever been a serial dater, unless you count the dates I've been on since my divorce from Grant and even then, there haven't been that many. I've mainly been in long-term relationships – four in total – and two of those resulted in marriage. Even when I was a teenager growing up in Stoke, I had a wide, mixed friendship group and my first proper boyfriend, a lovely guy, evolved from there. We went out for about a year until it fizzled out. He's in Sydney now and when I covered Australia Day for GMTV it was great to catch up with him and his family.

I met my second boyfriend Bruno Brooks through friends in a nightclub in Stoke when I was in my late teens. He did trials at Radio 1 as a DJ and then he got a long-term contract and moved to London to build his career. Around the same time I got offered a job in London too, working for a record company and we lived together for a while until the relationship stopped working and we split up.

Next was Peter Powell who became my husband years after we were first friends. We met through work really, Peter's company James Grant Management looked after my career for many years. I fell totally and completely in love with Pete and we were together for seven years. I adore him and we still have a close bond. I've purposely steered clear of explaining the reasons for our divorce out of respect for Pete but as we've never lost our friendship it couldn't have been that bad.

And finally along came Grant, who I'd known as a friend for several years before we fell in love. I first met him in 1990 when he brought some business to James Grant as he knew Pete's business partner, Russ Lindsay. The rest, as they say, is history. So the whole dating scene passed me by in a way which is why, when I found myself alone at fifty-three, I was absolutely petrified.

Everything I'd heard and witnessed told me dating, especially for an emotionally bruised woman of my age, was an absolute minefield and I didn't think I'd ever be able to cope. I mean, unless you already know someone or are introduced by a mutual friend, where do you meet a man these days? On the internet? Dating agencies? What's the difference between Tinder and Match.com? How can you tell if someone is genuine before you actually meet him? What if you hate him on sight or he hates you or he's married or wants nothing more than casual sex? Who pays for dinner? Who makes the first move? Then there's all the sexting and so-called d***-pics... Dating today appears to be so much more casual than I ever remember it being, people are much freer with their affections. I don't know the rules anymore or the whole protocol of going out with someone. What's the difference between dating and 'seeing' someone? Or between being exclusive and non-exclusive? I'm useless at all of it and it scares the life out of me!

Date, date, date!

Not long after Grant and I split up, a lot of my female friends insisted I 'get out there' and date, date, date! Jilly Johnson is an old friend who is amazing when it comes to men. She's ten years older than me and has been there, done it, lived it. She's no wall flower and would never shut herself off from life the way I was attempting to do. She told me to 'get out and go on as many dates as you can' her theory being throw as many balls at the wall as possible and one will stick. I'd not dated in forever and couldn't just throw myself into the lion's den the way she would. I'm sure a lot of women will relate to that but maybe I've just lived a sheltered life. It's terrifying. It's that fear of being rejected again, things not working out.

Me and Jilly promoting The Moon Walk for Breast Cancer.

© Brian Aris

Jilly's story

"When that piece of paper comes through the post and you're gleefully leaping into the air you think, this is it! This is my new life! But it's actually not as simple as that. There is a period of mourning after divorce and I do think we all have done this – at least I did – gone rushing out there, all available and ready to party. And party I did. I must have spent so many hours dancing on the table and dating quite unsuitable people I'd been set up with by my friends. Lots of blind dates. Those days of walking into a restaurant and seeing someone standing at the bar who would come up to my shoulder, looking quite shifty and decidedly dodgy and you think, please God no! If there's one man you don't want to be set up with, it's him and of course he turns out to be the one. This happened to me quite a few times by well-meaning friends.

I think one does, or I did, spend a lot of time rushing from pillar to post, from dates to parties. I think it's very much tears of a clown you know, making oneself so busy to avoid thinking about what was the past. It did take my mind off things because I was frantic the whole time, chasing my tail. I went to every party, every premiere known to man really, just to be out there and busy, rather than sitting at home. I think that is the way to do it, to be honest, you've got to go out there and go for it, live your life. I know it's not for everyone. Some people do take the period of mourning in a heartfelt way and I feel sad about that. Not everyone can dance on tables.

I didn't really have any good dates immediately after my divorce. I think it's because one is looking, even though people say they're not looking, believe me they are. Why would you want to go out with someone horrible or not your cup of tea? I met men mostly through friends. Once my son-in-law fixed me up because as he said, 'I don't want to get stuck with you in a granny annexe.' Fortunately, I do have a sense of humour. The date went shockingly badly and I said, 'You can't be that desperate to get shot of me!' I was horribly cowardly when it came to getting rid of men. I would just ignore their calls and hope that they got the message. I don't ever want to hurt anyone's feelings. I once left a date half way through the evening - it might have been the one my son-in-law set me up with - I legged it out the back door when he went to get us a drink. I don't want say too much about what was wrong with him because I don't want to sound heartless. I think it must have been a joke, after all, he was dribbling . . .

I did have a lot of interest from men, not always with good intentions. Once I met a man through a friend of a friend after he said he'd always wanted to meet me and had just heard I'd got divorced so I agreed. He claimed he was forty-four but when we met, it was obvious he couldn't have been a day younger than sixty. I was only in my thirties so it was quite a shock. There were several of those, men who turned out to be a lot older than they said.

I met my present husband again through a friend. I don't think it's easy to meet the right person in clubs to be honest. I'm very happily married now. I don't regret the fun I had after my divorce. I still say the best way to get over a man is to get under another. I think it takes your mind out of the whole equation. Even if it's a short lived romance, it's a good diversion."

The saying 'the best way to get over someone is to get under someone new' may sound clever but I'm not convinced the theory is a sound one. You can't use someone new as a sticking plaster in my opinion. You need to sort yourself out first before you are able to try and build a relationship with someone else.

About a year into being single once more, a friend of mine set me up with someone. I didn't really want to meet him but she convinced me I should make the effort. I recalled previously moaning to my friend, Sun columnist Jane Moore, 'No one asks me out.' She'd replied: 'Do you know why? Because you have "f*** off" tattooed across your forehead.' 'Oh.' So I thought I'd better try and stop being so closed off to the idea of romance and just go. What did I have to lose apart from one evening away from the telly?

I remember sitting there with this perfectly nice man, chatting and enjoying a meal in a pleasant restaurant in London. I wasn't feeling it but I'm very polite and would never have been rude enough to make it obvious. He was an engaging, talkative chap but there wasn't a spark there – at least from where I was sitting. Gradually, he began to inch his chair closer to mine, invading my personal space which I noticed with some surprise. But before I could edge back, he suddenly leant over and tried to kiss me. Instinctively, I literally dived in the opposite direction so I practically put my head under the table while he was left kissing the air! It was awful of me but it was honestly a knee-jerk reaction. It was massively awkward and needless to say, we didn't see each other again. I just knew then I couldn't deal with another dating episode with someone I didn't know. I had no inclination that night or any night for a long time afterwards. I'd been Anthea Turner: polite and pleasant but distant. That's no way in which to try and enter a new relationship which meant I simply wasn't ready. For some people, getting 'out there' works. It's definitely a distraction from the pain and loneliness of divorce but for me, it wasn't the kind of distraction I was ready for or one that I needed so soon after my break up.

"I signed up to three different dating agencies before the ink on my divorce papers was dry. The thought of staying in night after night on my own, while my ex moved on with his new partner, was too depressing for words. I still haven't met Mr Right but I've had so many adventures, I could write a book! I know there's someone out there for me and I'm determined to find him."

Clara, 36.

"My first dating experience after my divorce was a disaster, the man was a creep! We met for a drink in a busy wine bar near London Bridge after we got talking on a dating site called Zeus and I had high hopes we'd hit it off. Wrong. Not only was he a good fifteen years older than his picture suggested, but he was clearly after just one thing. After a quick drink, he suggested we leave and find a nearby hotel because he had to be home by 10pm! I did leave – alone – and didn't bother saying goodbye. I'm pleased to say I've had better luck since and have been seeing a lovely guy for almost a year."

Debbie, 53.

As you can probably tell, my experiences are not going to help you very much if you're hoping to learn about how to meet the perfect man after your divorce. As I write, dating again is still a subject I approach with trepidation. But what I can say with some certainty, is look out for the warning signs when it comes to meeting a new partner. Look at their patterns of behaviour when getting to know them and don't ignore any red flags. For example, if his relationship history is littered with short, failed partnerships, the chances are that he's the problem and not the women he's dated. Is he still bitter and antagonistic towards his ex-wife? If the answer's yes, another red flag is waving at you. If he's say in his fifties and still not solvent, and blames everyone else for his failures another red flag.

You need someone who's going to improve your life, not complicate it even further. And if after you've been seeing someone for a while, you still haven't met his family or friends, ask yourself why not. You can tell a lot about a person from the company they keep and their relationships with loved ones. If he doesn't get on with his nearest and dearest and appears to have very few people he calls good friends, again, maybe he's the problem. Another warning sign you can't afford to ignore.

I've already talked at length in earlier chapters about the grief and loneliness of divorce and I appreciate it can be very tempting to try and fill the gap with someone else. Friends who urged me to find a new man after my divorce meant well. They could see I was struggling at times and how much I hated rocking up to events on my own. Worse still, leaving alone at the end of the evening and returning to an empty apartment. But despite the dark moments and feelings of despair, I knew in my heart that I had to learn to live by myself and feel comfortable with my new status before genuinely ready to start something new. There's no rush, it's not a race. I'm a little spiritual about this area of my life and I know the universe will bring the right person in when the time is right for both of us.

The other day a friend called and one of her first questions was, 'How's your love life?' I was actually a bit miffed by that. Why don't you ask me how I am, what I've been doing? Why does there always have to a man involved? I actually got quite evangelical about it. Admittedly I wasn't having a good day so I may have over reacted slightly but I realised I don't wish to be defined by a relationship and that's a positive thing. I'm absolutely fine being me. I'm pursing my social interests, my business interests and my friendships, both male and female. For now that's plenty.

DATING AGAIN

A much happier me today.

© Alison Webster

Chapter Eight
And Now...

There's nothing worse than people who continually invite you to a pity party, over and over again. It gets tedious and boring. There has to come a time when no matter what you've been through, it is what it is and you move on. I don't have terminal cancer, I have a lovely family and great friends so I appreciate I have nothing to complain about any longer.

If you're still reading this book and have reached this the final part of the journey, I do hope you've learnt from it and taken something helpful from my experiences and the other women who've shared their stories. I've tried to be as honest and as open as I can and shared with you all the things that I've been taught and learnt along the well-trodden path to life-after-divorce.

It has not been easy and it has nothing to do with how much money you do or don't have or how big your house is; this is about life and feelings and we all hurt in the same way. Having spoken to friends and colleagues who've been through painful break-ups, we're probably all damaged in some way, big or small, especially me. But as I've stressed already in many of the pages of this book, it's about eventually letting go of the hurt and unloading those feelings for good. By the time you've reached the point in your life that I have, you'll know that the worst thing you can do to yourself is to hold on to destructive emotions. There will be times of course when even now, something – perhaps a song or a familiar place – triggers a poignant memory of days gone by and you feel a stab of pain and maybe even shed a tear. But I promise you that by now, those trigger moments will be few and far between. And when they do crop up, you need to find the strength to swipe them away.

As women, we always urge each other to talk to our girlfriends about the way we're feeling. I for one have a tendency to share everything generally and my heartache was no exception. Look how much I've shared in this book! But there comes a time when you need to stop talking about it, stop sharing every spit and cough about your ex, how much he's wounded you, what he's been up... Once you've vented, once you've purged, it's time to call a halt to sharing once and for all. Trust me, I know from experience that with some effort it is possible. There's something extremely unattractive about a person who is full of bitterness about their previous partner, no matter who was at fault and who did what to whom. My dyslexic brain sees everything in pictures. I imagine myself with this big bag into which I've stuffed every toxic, sad and miserable thought and simply walked away. Now when people see me and ask how I am, I give them a brief explanation and no more. I have other things to talk about. My marriage is in the past and outside of the girls and the purposes of this book I don't want to revisit those days. Spiritually it's referred to as good or bad energy and from now on, I choose to keep my life full of good energy.

Everyone has their own way of dealing with things I appreciate, and I have been able to share only what works for me and women I've spoken to. If you meet a man and all he talks about is his ex, years after his divorce, it's draining and that bad energy will bring you down. Or if you bump into an old friend and she is full of negativity, you're not going to be in a rush to meet up again. So think about that the next time you're trying to forge a relationship with a potential partner or are chatting to pals: are you being bright, positive and a joy to be around, or are you bringing them down with your sob stories?

I know I have delved back into my past in order to write this book and believe me, it's been hard going at times. I've found myself in tears more than once. But I did it for good reason: I want to help others in a similar position to the one in which I found myself. Now that I've come to the end of my story so far, I can assure you, I have moved on with my life and hopefully you have or will do too. There is nothing worse than a person living in the past, wallowing in her own misery and I knew I didn't want to be that person. I am not that person!

My good friend Clare went through a scenario not that dissimilar to mine. She gave her cheating ex a second chance – he blew it – and like me, was forced to carve out a new life for herself afterwards. She's now blissfully happy and successful, an inspiration. I'm delighted she agreed to share her story here. The older you get, the more you can see your own mortality. You owe it to yourself to achieve as much as you can in the time you have left. I genuinely believe it takes three to four years to completely reach this point. Well, it did for me. I'm now back to being Anthea Turner. I'm happy, contented and looking forward to the future and all the possibilities it holds. I truly couldn't imagine saying that in 2013!

"Attitude is a choice.
Happiness is a choice. Optimism is a choice.
Kindness is a choice. Giving is a choice. Respect
is a choice. Whatever choice you make makes
you. Choose wisely."
– Roy T. Bennett, The Light in the Heart.

Clare's story...

"It was at my thirtieth birthday party when the truth struck me, blinding me – like a bright white light. My then husband, and childhood sweetheart was not only sleeping with my colleague's wife, but was also dabbling in narcotics. His perfectly snub nose was laced with white powder as he left the toilets to rejoin the party and head back to continue flirting with who I soon found out was his latest conquest.

It was like someone had suddenly removed the blinkers from eyes and I could no longer hide from the truth. My relationship of fourteen years was no longer what I thought it was – things had changed, and I could no longer control the course we were on.

I thought I was desperately in love at the time (little did I know it was just puppy love in its strongest form) so once I could breathe again, I chose to fight. To fight for the life I had chosen and thought was forever. I knew my partner wasn't perfect, in fact he had been quite a tough person to live with, struggling to find his role in life and suffering from agoraphobia at one point. Well, the white stuff had certainly seemed to cure that. . . for the time being at least. He had a new found confidence and swagger and a steeliness in his eyes that was unrecognisable to me, and looking back, I never properly connected with those eyes again after that moment. But boy did I try! I'm not one to accept failure and I was determined to get things back on the rails. Perhaps I had let myself go and was to blame for all this?

So when he left me some weeks later, I set about losing weight, getting fit, getting a sun tan, and pretending to be carefree. I went on holiday, got a promotion and all the while pretended to the rest of the world we were fine, this was just a blip. I even lied about him moving out to those that I could. He was 'away with work' or 'visiting family' – I was in total denial. But a few short months later he did indeed beg to return and to patch things up. Eventually we agreed to paper over the cracks and carry on, as if nothing had happened and I felt nothing but relief.

At first I kidded myself it was like putting back on those comfy slippers. He was young, he was bound to want to taste the forbidden fruit – he was only twenty-nine after all! At last I was back on the course that I knew and felt comfortable with. But we all know that when you paper over cracks they just re-appear in a different place.

One night we went to a friend's birthday party at their swish pad in Cheshire. We arrived early and it was a sunny evening so we all sat in the garden. Being the person I am and have always been, it wasn't long before I had seventy year-old granny on the trampoline with me and later in the night I was giving the host a run for her money on the karaoke machine. All the while my ex sat in corners, nipping off to the bathroom and lurking in shadows. By 1am the final guests were leaving and our hosts were sat in their pyjamas when I suggested we leave too – only to be told back at our hotel that I was a total bore and had dragged him away from the party too early. What! I later learned this is what is professionally known as 'transference'. My ex was a shy person who hadn't found a career path and was jumping from job to job to try to find the right fit. I, on the other hand, was confident and bubbly and had flourished in an exciting career that I loved. We had grown apart without me realising and as he eventually confessed, he 'lived in my shadow'.

I tried again to change things and even found him a job in my industry but within months the rumours were rife that he was sleeping with someone on my team. . .a girl ten years younger than me and at least ten pounds lighter! He had chosen to bite the hand that fed him and when I finally reeled from the gossips and realisation that he had done it to me again, I closed the door once and for all on what had become a painful chapter of guilt and pretence.

It was so tough to walk away from fourteen years of childhood friendship, the future had seemed so bright, but I had been made a fool of not once, but twice – so who was the real fool here? It was quite clever looking back that he backed me into a corner where I had to be the one to end things – I had no choice.

Within a year I had quit my job and moved to Los Angeles. I wasn't rich - I sold my car and a few precious possessions to do it - but I couldn't stay around all the dirty laundry both at home and at work. So I ran away. I didn't know a soul in LA and had travelled there with work just once before – but it seemed like a land of opportunity and right now, that was all I needed. Of course by this time I was still only thirty-one with no kids – so this adventure was open to me, and for many I appreciate it's not. But whether it's emigrating, or just changing a circle of friends, I truly believe you have to make real changes in your lifestyle in order to move on.

I just chose to do it 6,000 miles away.

It seems like a cliché but if I could only have told that brave young woman what I know now – not that she would have listened – but my divorce turned out to be the best thing that ever happened to me. Truly. My life had been headed on a path of looking after someone else – not just financially, but emotionally too. I had been trying to fix someone, to take them on my journey in the hope it would make them happy – but of course it didn't. Consequently I lived in a constant state of guilt, playing down my work achievements and missing out on things in order to keep the peace at home.

Now it was time to spread my wings and live only for myself – what a luxury. After some therapy and a lot of tears, I built a new life in the sunshine. Of course it wasn't long before my true Prince Charming arrived – and this time he WAS the right fit. Relaxed, confident, self-made, kind and funny. Yep, I got it all. Today I live back in England with him and our two kids in what I can only describe as a perfect life – well it's perfect for me. I now realise that my divorce was the cloud that brought about the silver lining in my life and I thank God for it regularly. I shudder at the thought of what might have happened if we had clambered along into old age in a relationship that wasn't right for either of us. Luckily we were brave enough to stop the car and say 'actually, this journey isn't for me after all'. It takes bravery and a smidgeon of madness, but I truly believe it can be the best move you ever make, it certainly was for me."

AND NOW...

So, what is life like for me now? I've already confessed about my dating experiences — or lack of. But it doesn't mean I intend staying single forever. I know for sure that I don't have any need for time wasters and idiots and neither should you. In our fifties we all have baggage but what I now look for is someone who has worked hard to deal with it. I have a huge respect for people who've had really difficult times but have strived to overcome their problems. I personally have worked really hard with dealing with my own wounds, and I don't carry a lot of emotional baggage anymore. I think often women do deal with it because we're not afraid to do so, whereas a lot of men — and I know I'm generalising here and it's wrong of me — are afraid to confront personal issues. We women are not afraid to seek help, we're not afraid to talk to our friends. We know if we don't sort things out, there will be consequences and no one wants 'bitter and twisted' stamped across their forehead. It is vitally important that whatever means you need and use to deal with it, deal with it, otherwise you are doing a disservice to yourself as a human being. I know several men that carry problems in terms of issues they've never resolved. They can't deal with real life because they've shoved so much under the carpet that the carpet's come off the gripper rod. I said to somebody only yesterday, 'You've got more hang ups than an Indian call centre and it doesn't do you any favours!' He laughed but he agreed that I was right. Will he do something about it? Who knows.

Another post-divorce family celebration.

AND NOW...

As for Grant, I've talked at length about him. No one can be in any doubt about how much he's hurt me. But he's the father of Amelia, Lily and Claudia and even though I'm not their biological Mum, for their sake if no one else's, he remains an important part of my life today.

I feel we are all defined by our relationships with others — our family, friends and children. I judge people on their relationships and I pride myself not on my career, but on my personal relationships, especially with my step-daughters, which has reached a place that cannot be altered. We have a strong bond and we're all grateful for it. I have firm contact with my ex's family because they are all part of the girls also. It's an unbroken chain. Consequently, I have a good relationship with Grant because he's the girls' father and an important and integral part of their lives. I acknowledge that we did share some happy times and have both good and bad memories which I can't and don't want to erase.

I knew pretty early on that if I decided to cut off all contact with Grant after our divorce that I could be the one who ended up suffering the most. We both have years ahead of us to share in some wonderful occasions with the girls such as weddings, birthdays and Christenings and as I've said before, I didn't want to run the risk of missing out on anything. I didn't want to put the girls in the position of having to choose between us or to feel awkward about whom to invite where. It's taken a lot of tongue-biting at times and some deep breaths (on my part anyway) but we're now in a good place. It's better for us and it's better for the family, especially Amelia, Lily and Claudia. Friends have asked if it's stressful or difficult being together on these social occasions and I can tell them in all honesty that it's actually not. If the girls are happy then so am I and I think Grant feels the same.

We both have our own lives now and he's no longer the first person I rush to call when something happens. There was a time when I wouldn't have made a decision without him but now I make my own choices, good or bad. I wouldn't block myself off from another long-term and fulfilling relationship, it's clearly my default setting, but I'm happy being me these days. If you're defined by your relationship as I admit I was, and it all goes wrong, then who are you? I'm no longer co-dependent. I wouldn't block myself off from another long-term and fulfilling relationship but I'm happy being me these days.

When I first started out on my divorce journey, reaching this point seemed a long, long way away, even impossible. I spent years talking a good story but deep down, I secretly didn't believe I'd actually get here. Depending on where you started it can take years but get here you will. Boy, are you a happier, stronger, more considered and spiritual human being when you arrive! My empathy for others and their problems is sharper. You read a lot these days about EQ (emotional intelligence) which supersedes IQ and I would say I have a First Class Honours in EQ from the University of Life. (My IQ is always open to debate!) Maybe when you're younger and GCSEs, A Levels and so on are all-important but they become slightly less so as you grow older. What you need is EQ. Some sadly, is learnt the hard way, having experienced the ups and downs of what life throws at us.

I've had some chaotic times and I'm grateful for them all. For all my mistakes, I've learnt to be a much better person. I know there are people who can't bear to talk to their exes because there's too much residual bitterness but I've found that unless someone has been abusive, it's actually easier to keep communicating. Grant and I can have perfectly good conversations. It would be easy for either of us to wander off down a tributary road with a hazard warning sign flashing, raking up the past and causing rows. If you feel yourself turning down that road, stop! Ask yourself, 'Who's going to get upset by this?' You, of course. So don't go down there, no good will come of resurrecting old grievances. We do have to be strong with ourselves and have the confidence not to veer off-course. I can never regret my relationship with Grant because of the girls. Those years we spent together as husband and wife were interesting and at times exciting, quite an adventure. Materially I gained a lot and lost a lot, although is it a loss? They are only 'things'. I have the girls and I have my sanity and as a human being, if we're on this earth to learn, I have learnt.

It is quite amazing that when you let the bad things out of your life, the good stuff comes through. As I sit here now, I have a full diary, both with social and work events. I've got a lot to look forward to and I'm very thankful. I've still got my hang ups about going on holiday alone but I've got to get over that one! Life has definitely turned a sunny corner for me and I thank the Lord that barring any health issues, I'm back on my feet.

I'm now in control of all aspects of my life. Never again will I allow anyone to take financial control. It's all down to me now. I may not have a house any more but I don't care! I have a lovely flat which is mine and who knows, one day I may be able to move to a house once again through my own hard work. And if not, so what? What's important is that I'm happy and confident once more and I'm back to making my own decisions.

When I think back, when mistakes were made, it's because I didn't listen to me. One of my favourite phrases is 'life makes more sense backwards' and it's so true! Always listen to your inner self; it's the one that makes the wise decisions, the one that's not wrong. We women have a heightened intuition but we often push it away and don't listen to it enough even though we should.

Take this everyday scenario: when I'm on the London underground with a friend, we're chatting away and if it's a complicated journey (they often can be) we share the responsibility of our destination and sometimes we just assume the other knows where they're going. The amount of times I've done this and we've both got lost! On my own it's down to me, I'm focused, I've worked out my route, I concentrate on where I'm heading and rarely go wrong. This is how I try to live all my life now. Because of everything that has happened in the last few years, my emotional and practical mind has never been as sharp as it is today.

While I'm a wiser woman these days, I will always follow my heart, I always have done, although I know now that I will listen to my head much more too! I have always said that I never want to snuggle up to a pile of VHSs of my greatest moments in television, which means in my world, real life wins. I would say that most of the decisions I've made in my life have been for personal and emotional reasons and my heart has absolutely, definitely, always ruled my head. When I look back I see the pattern of my behaviour has consistently been related to my love-life, right from when I first came to London with my then boyfriend.

Later on, I gave up presenting a successful television show – *Wish You Were Here* – in order to focus on my new life with Grant. I did the show for about three years and absolutely loved it but it meant that I would spend six months of my year travelling and filming and that's not conducive to a successful relationship. It's certainly not conducive to bonding with three young step daughters. I needed to be at home in order to make this newly constructed family work. I'd put my head above the parapet, made this huge decision and I thought I'd work the rest out. And that's what I did. I spent the rest of the years of my marriage, putting a lot of effort into making it work. No regrets.

As I sit here now, I still believe real life wins because when we're all lying there, a lot older, I think we remember people and think about relationships. When I speak to elderly people, what they talk about is not their work but the people that have meant most to them. That's what you carry in your heart, not your job; I firmly believe that. If you're ever away from home, and I spent a lot of time away, what do you think about? You think about family and you think about your friends. It's all about people.

But I have to say, because now I'm in my mid-fifties, I have to think carefully about the years I have left. I have more behind me than I have in front of me and I don't want to ruin them with more mistakes. We're all older and wiser, especially after something as traumatic and life changing as a divorce and it would be very silly if we didn't pull on our experiences and learn from them. We all need to make some wise decisions going forward.

A good friend recently reminded me how lucky I am and I think she's right. I'm still young and enthusiastic enough to start over and that's just what I'm doing, but with more wisdom and consideration. After all the hurt, betrayal and pain, I'm finally happy once more. Writing this book has helped me and if you get this far, I do hope it has helped you too.

Useful
Contacts

British Association for Counselling & Psychotherapy
www.bacp.co.uk

British Psychological Society, The
www.bps.org.uk

Citizens Advice Bureau
www.citizensadvice.org.uk

Family Law Association, The (Scotland)
www.familylawassociation.org

Dr Karen Finn, Divorce Coach
www.drkarenfinn.com

1st For Mediation, Donna Goodwin, Family Mediator
www.1stformediation.co.uk 0800 612 5272

Grosvenor Law, Tracey Rodford
www.grosvenorlaw.com 020 3189-4200

Sarah Jones, Life Coach
www.sarahjonesuk.com

Law Society of Northern Ireland, The
www.lawsoc-ni.org

Morrisons Solicitors LLP, Anne-Lise Wall

www.morrlaw.com 01737 854500

National Domestic Violence Helpline

www.nationaldomesticviolencehelpline.org.uk

0808 2000-247

Positive Group

www.positivegroup.org

0207 936-3454

Relate

www.relate.org.uk

0300 100-1234

Resolution (England and Wales)

www.resolution.org.uk.

Tavistock Centre for Couple Relationships

www.tccr.org.uk

0207 380-1975

Useful
Reading

Emotional Intelligence 2.0
Travis Bradberry & Jean Greaves

The Magic
Rhonda Byrne

The Power
Rhonda Byrne

The Secret
Rhonda Byrne

Depressive Illness, The Curse of the Strong
Dr Tim Cantopher

Being Human
Steve Chalke

Happily Ever After...An Essential Guide to Successful Relationships
Janet Clegg and Hilary Browne-Wilkinson

After The Affair: How to Build Trust and Love Again
J.Cole

Mindset
Dr Carol S. Dweck

The Compassionate Mind

Paul Gilbert

Everything You Need You Have

Gerad Kite

The Compassionate Mind Approach to Recovering From Trauma

Deborah Lee with Sophie James

Fast Asleep Wide Awake

Dr Nerina Ramlakhan

Index

Also available from Splendid Publications

William and Kate's Britain -
An Insider's Guide to the haunts of the Duke and Duchess of
Cambridge
By Claudia Joseph

Britain is an island with a rich cultural heritage, which dates back
to the Roman era: it is a land of pubs and football; rock music
and opera; historic palaces and village churches; breath-taking
scenery and ancient monuments. That's not to mention its
spectacular pageantry – the royal wedding ceremony at St Paul's
Cathedral and the Queen's Diamond Jubilee celebrations were
beamed to billions around the world. Now, in a unique guide
to the British Isles, royal author Claudia Joseph goes behind the
scenes – and reveals the secrets – of William and Kate's Britain.

£9.99 (paperback)

Daniel, My Son -
A Father's Powerful Account Of His Son's Cancer Journey
By David Thomas

Daniel was just 17, rich of talent and full of dreams, when he received
the devastating news that he had bone cancer all over his body. In
pain and facing horrific treatment, his chances were slim. But Daniel
refused to give up on life and studied Classics at Oxford, played with
the BBC Symphony Orchestra, line-judged at Wimbledon and was
chosen to carry the Olympic Torch.
 Meanwhile his heartbroken parents scoured the world for a cure and
learnt to navigate the medical maze. Their mission was to create hope
– for Daniel, themselves and all those facing the same nightmare: a
child with cancer. This is a father's powerful story of his love for his
son and humankind's overriding need for hope.

£7.99 (paperback)

The Old Fart's Guide to Survival
By Dawn Cawley

Dawn Cawley, a paid-up member of The Old Fart's Club, certainly isn't ready to be put out to pasture just yet and shares her tips and observations on life in the slow lane.

From dealing with modern technology and grandkids, to old friendships and going deaf, this quirky and humorous take on later life, is a must-have survival guide for all the Old Farts who aim to grow old(er) disgracefully!

£4.99 (paperback)

FREE
DELIVERY
ON ALL
ORDERS

Order online at:
www.splendidpublications.co.uk